Published in 2017 by The School of Life
70 Marchmont Street, London WC1N 1AB
Copyright © The School of Life 2017
Designed and typeset by FLOK, Berlin
Printed in Latvia by Livonia Print

A proportion of this book has appeared online at thebookoflife.org.

Every effort has been made to contact the copyright holders of the material
reproduced in this book. If any have been inadvertently overlooked, the publisher
will be pleased to make restitution at the earliest opportunity.

The School of Life offers programmes, publications and services to assist modern
individuals in their quest to live more engaged and meaningful lives. We've
also developed a collection of content-rich, design-led retail products to promote
useful insights and ideas from culture.

www.theschooloflife.com

ISBN 978-0-9957535-9-4

10 9 8 7 6 5 4

The School of Life Dictionary

The Language of Emotional Intelligence

Contents

Introduction

A dictionary is a guide to language. This is a dictionary for the distinctive language that the School of Life 'speaks', which is that of emotions. It is a selection of words and phrases that sheds light on our feelings about ourselves, other people and the workings of the modern world.

Too often, we're left fighting for a way to explain our emotional intentions; this dictionary is a tool to help us convey our meanings with economy and precision.

The School of Life is an organisation with a simple mission: to increase the amount of Emotional Intelligence in circulation. We seek more emotionally intelligent kinds of relationships, workplaces, economies and culture.

What structures our thinking – found in the dictionary entries in the pages ahead – are eight central themes, which unfold as follows:

1. Self-Knowledge

Socrates, the earliest and greatest of philosophers, summed up the purpose of philosophy in one resonant phrase: 'know yourself'. A capacity for self-knowledge is at the heart of our inclinations to forgiveness, kindness, creativity and wise decision-making, especially around love and work. Unfortunately, knowing ourselves is the (always unfinished) task of a lifetime. We are permanently elusive and mysterious to ourselves. We have to catch our real intentions and feelings obliquely, with some of the patience of a lepidopterist.

One of the tasks of culture is to offer us tools to assist us with the task of self-knowledge. We need a vocabulary to name feelings and states of mind; we need encouragement to be alone with ourselves at regular moments; we need friends and professionals who will listen to us with editorial precision and sympathy, and we need works of art that can illuminate elusive aspects of our psyches.

Above all, we need to be modest about our capacity easily to understand who we are and what we want. We should nurture a stance of scepticism towards many of our first impulses and beliefs and submit all our significant plans to extensive rational cross-examination.

Failures of self-knowledge lie behind some of our gravest individual and collective disasters.

2. Other People

Having to live around other people can severely challenge any desire to remain calm, kind and good. The School of Life takes seriously the ambition of being polite and nice, despite the lack of prestige that surrounds these concepts and the constant frictions and misunderstandings that attend communal life.

At The School of Life, we also know that kindness is a skill that has to be learnt – and that we must put unexpectedly intense energy into the task of overcoming our first responses to other people, which often veer (quite understandably) towards rage, paranoia and defensiveness.

Two manoeuvres stand out. We must expect less of people – not in order to do an injustice to them, but so as to be readier to forgive and accept problems when they arise. And we must learn to see that bad behaviour almost always stems not from evil but from pain and anxiety. We need to direct sympathy and imagination towards a very unfamiliar target: those who frustrate us most.

3. Relationships

Relationships are perhaps our single greatest source of both happiness and suffering. Unlike people in previous ages, we don't merely seek a partner we can tolerate; we seek someone we can love, usually over many decades, at an intense pitch of desire, commitment and interest. We dream of someone who will understand us, with whom we can share our longings and our secrets, and with whom we can properly be ourselves.

Then the horror begins. We need to understand why. Some of it is because our childhoods leave us with a legacy of trouble around relating to others. We have difficulties trusting or being close, achieving the right distance or staying resilient. We cannot comfortably express what we feel, and are prone to 'transfer' a lot of emotions from the past on to present-day scenarios where they don't quite belong.

We need to chart our own psyches and offer maps of our madness to partners early on, before we have had the chance to hurt them too much with our behaviour.

Our current relationship difficulties stem in part from a cultural source that we call 'Romanticism'. In the background, we operate with a deeply problematic Romantic picture of what good relationships should be like: we dream of profound intimacy, satisfying sex, an absence of secrets and only a modicum of conflict. This faith in love is touching, but it carries with it a tragic flaw: our expectations turn out to be the enemies of workable mature relationships.

At The School of Life, we are drawn to what we call a Classical approach to love. The Classical view is in certain ways cautious. Classical people pay special attention to what can go wrong around others. Before condemning a relationship, they consider the standard of partners across society and may interpret a current arrangement as bearable, under the circumstances. This view of people is fundamentally, but usefully, dark. Ultimately, everyone is deeply troubled and hard to live with. The only people we can think of as normal are those we don't know very well.

4. Sexuality

At the School of Life, we are aware of the scale of the hopes and challenges around sex. Although we often believe ourselves to be living in a liberated age, it remains difficult not to feel shame around many of our sexual impulses. It is especially tricky to communicate what we want to those we are drawn to.

The School of Life believes in laying out a sober understanding of what drives desire and in removing some of the shame around fantasies, revealing that many of our more outlandish wishes belong to complex quests for intimacy.

5. Work

One of the distinctive ideas of modern times is that we don't expect work to be simply a drudgery that we have to undertake to survive. We have high expectations of this huge part of our lives. Ideally, we want work to be 'meaningful', which involves the belief that we are in some way either reducing the pain or increasing the happiness of other humans.

Three big reasons stand out for why meaningful work has become difficult to secure:

Firstly, it is perilously hard for us to locate our true interests in the time we have before sheer survival becomes an imperative. Our interests don't manifest themselves spontaneously; they require us to patiently analyse ourselves and try out a range of options, to see what feels like the best 'fit' for us. Unfortunately, schools and universities, as well as society at large, don't place much emphasis on helping people to understand their authentic working identities. There is far more stress on simply getting ready for any job as opposed to identifying a job that would be particularly well suited to us. This is a pity – not just for individuals, but for the economy as a whole – because people work more imaginatively and more fruitfully when their deep selves are engaged.

Secondly, many jobs are relatively meaningless because it's very possible, in the current economy, to generate profits from selling people things that don't fundamentally contribute to well-being, but prey instead on their appetites and lack of self-command.

Thirdly, a job may have real meaning while not feeling as if it does day to day because many organisations are so large, so slow-moving, and so split up over continents that the purpose of everyone's work gets lost amid meetings, memos, conference calls and administration.

This diagnosis helps to point the way to how we could make work more meaningful:

Firstly, pay a lot more attention to helping people find their vocation – their authentic working selves.

Secondly, the more we, as customers, support businesses engaged in meaningful work, the more meaningful jobs there will be. By raising the quality of demand, we raise the number of occupations that answer to humanity's deeper needs.

Thirdly, in businesses that do carry out meaningful work, but on too large a scale over too long a period for it to feel meaningful, there is scope to narrate stories of the organisation's purpose that offer a more tangible sense of every individual's contribution to the whole.

Ensuring that work is meaningful is no luxury. It determines the greatest issue of all in modern economics: how contentedly and how skilfully people will work – and therefore how successful and fruitful societies can be.

6. Capitalism

Economies look as if they are driven by huge material elements, as if they are about oil fields, communications satellites, huge retail complexes and vast entertainment districts. But behind these impressive factors, the economy is, to an extraordinary extent, a psychological phenomenon driven by our collective appetites, imaginations and longings. What we call capitalism is, in the end, the result of the way our minds work.

Up till now, capitalism has tended to focus on supplying our more basic needs. The School of Life is interested in a kind of capitalism that can target higher needs: that is, a capitalism that is as efficient at meeting our needs for understanding as for sweet things to eat; that is as great at helping us live wisely as it is adept at uniting us with the ideal confectionery or garment.

The task is to expand the economy so as to help it engage with humanity's real internal issues, which have usually lain outside the area of commerce as commonly defined.

7. Culture

People who want to express admiration for culture often say it is valuable 'for its own sake'. We propose that it is valuable because of its capacity to address our needs for education, guidance, consolation, perspective, encouragement and correction.

The School of Life is drawn to the idea that culture is therapeutic. This doesn't mean it should primarily help us with very urgent mental health issues. However, it can assist us with managing the normal troubles of everyday life: the tendency to become irritated with people we like; to lose perspective over minor matters; to abandon sympathy for people who deserve our compassion; and to take too harsh a view of our own mistakes.

The School of Life believes that the world has, up to now, not properly made use of the true therapeutic potential of culture, paying it reverence without learning how to make use of it systematically.

8. Religion

The School of Life is both a secular organisation and interested in many of the moves of religions. Some faith-based ideas (for example, the claim that the soul can be reincarnated, that Christ rose from the dead or that the creator of the cosmos made specific promises about land rights at the eastern end of the Mediterranean) have clouded some highly important psychological practices that religions were adept at promoting. Religions have been machines for addressing a range of important emotional needs, which endure even into a scientific era.

At their best, religions tried to keep ideas about forgiveness at the front of our minds; encouraged compassion; insisted that certain forms of worldly success were misleading ways of assessing the worth of people; got us to recognise our own capacities to hurt others and to feel sorry for doing so; nudged us to be tender and understanding towards the secret sufferings of others; and gave us helpful rituals and beautiful works of culture to keep important ideas before us throughout the year.

We see The School of Life as picking up many of the tasks of religion and creating secular substitutes for a range of religious ideals and practices. We believe in the idea that culture can and should replace scripture.

* * *

This organisation is, ultimately, a school that believes that the ability to learn is one of the most basic things about human beings. The range of things that we can learn to do better, via instruction, is very wide – far wider than we tend to think.

The powerful influence of Romanticism, which is convinced that better emotional responses cannot be taught, means the current education system fails to pass emotional intelligence down the generations as it should.

The School of Life takes the more Classical view that all important human achievements, especially around emotions, can be transmitted: how to control rage; how to have a conversation; how to be a loving parent; how to be calmer or less inclined to bitterness.

Nevertheless, we at The School of Life are aware of how easily people are turned off by anything that appears too preachy and by a fatal tendency for what is worthy to come across as dull. Our commitment to education makes us profoundly interested in the task of seduction: the need to get and hold people's attention artfully in a highly individualistic world filled with distractions and demands.

Because education is so central, The School of Life is ambitious about what learning should be like. It should not only be children who go to school. All adults should see themselves as in need of education pretty much every day. One should never be done with school. One should stay an active student, learning throughout life. In the adult section of schools, there should be courses on how to converse with strangers or how to deal with the fear of getting old; how to calm down and how to forgive. Schools should be where a whole community gets educated, not just a place for children. Some classes should have seven-year-olds learning alongside fifty-year-olds (the two cohorts having been found to have equivalent maturities in a given area). In the Utopia, the phrase 'I've finished school' would sound extremely strange.

What follows are the key words and terms that underpin the project of emotional education to which we have given the name: The School of Life.

¶ Addiction

We operate with some stock images of the addict: a person with a heroin needle in a park, or who nurses a bottle of gin in a paper bag at nine in the morning, or who sneaks off at every opportunity to light up another joint of marijuana.

However dramatic and tragic such cases of addiction might be, they are simultaneously hugely reassuring to most of us – because they locate the addict far from ordinary experience, somewhere off-stage, in the land of semi-criminality and outright breakdown.

The School of Life defines addiction in another way: as the manic reliance on something, anything, to keep our darker or more unsettling thoughts and feelings at bay. What properly indicates addiction is not what someone is addicted to, because we can get addicted to pretty much anything. It is the motives behind a reliance on a certain element – and, in particular, our attachment to it as a way of avoiding encounters with the contents of our own minds and hearts.

For most of us, facing up to ourselves is a deeply anxiety-inducing prospect. We are filled with thoughts we don't want to entertain and feelings we are desperate not to feel. There is an infinite amount that we are angry and sad about that it would take an uncommon degree of courage to face. We experience a host of fantasies and desires that we have a huge incentive to disavow because of the extent to which they violate our self-image and our more normative commitments.

We should not pride ourselves because we aren't injecting something into our veins. Almost certainly, we are doing something else to take us away from ourselves. We are checking the news at four-minute intervals to keep the news from ourselves at bay. We're doing sport, exhausting our bodies in the hope of not having to hear from our minds. We're using work to get away from the true internal work that we're shirking.

To overcome addiction, we need to lose our fear of our minds. We need a collective sense of safety around confronting loss, humiliation, sexual desire and sadness.

On the other side of addiction is philosophy – understood as the patient, unfrightened, compassionate examination of the contents of our minds.

See also: Faulty Walnut, The; Monasteries; News from Within; Overeating; Philosophical Meditation; Unprocessed Emotion.

¶ Advertising

Adverts wouldn't work as powerfully as they do if they didn't operate with a very good sense of what our real needs are and what we really require in order to live good lives. Their emotional pull is based on their wise understanding that we are creatures who hunger not so much for material goods as for sexual love, good family relationships, connections with others and the feeling that we are respected. Advertisers build their most compelling campaigns by tapping into their intimate knowledge of our psyches.

An advert for a car might not tell us much about the quality of the suspension or the technology that went into the metallic paint because it realises that such things (mostly) don't touch our souls. Instead it shows us what we really want: a family coping well with the ups and downs of life or a dignified grey-haired man who knows how to greet the challenges of existence with stoic strength. An advert for jewellery will mainly be about a couple who are still close after ten years of marriage; a chocolate bar or a cashmere jumper might be brought to our notice by means of a touching evocation of friendship.

This approach can look cynical, but there is a touch of tragedy in the situation – the tragedy that our manufacturers lag so far behind our advertisers. These manufacturers know how to make rather good car suspensions and can produce utterly reliable timepieces; the jumpers may be elegant and the chocolate delicious. However, none of these manufacturers make much headway in delivering the things we really would love to be getting: the good family life, the self-belief, the warm marriage and the better friendships that currently painfully elude us and whose exquisite portrayal cleverly tricked us (perhaps) into buying a sedan or a barbecue set.

In a stern mood, we might think that, in an ideal society, advertisers would be banned from hinting that the right bag or oven-ready meal could help us to find love and companionship. But the real solution goes in a different direction. We should want manufacturers and businesses to become much more ambitious about solving our real problems and to generate products that might actually help us with our big, underlying longings.

In most adverts, the pains and the hopes of our lives have been superbly identified, but the products on the shelves remain almost comically at odds with our real needs. The task is not to ban advertisements but to create an economy that lives up to their deepest promises.

See also: Glamour; Good Business; Good Demand; Higher Needs; Utopia.

¶ Akrasia

A central problem of our minds is that we know so much in theory about how we should behave, but engage so little with our knowledge in our day-to-day conduct.

We know in theory about not eating too much, being kind, getting to bed early, focusing on our opportunities before it is too late, showing charity and remembering to be grateful. Yet in practice, our wise ideas have a notoriously weak ability to motivate our actual behaviour. Our knowledge is embedded within us and yet is ineffective for us.

The Ancient Greeks were unusually alert to this phenomenon and gave it a helpfully resonant name: *akrasia*, commonly translated as 'weakness of will'. It is because of akrasia, they proposed, that we have such a tragic proclivity for knowing what to do but not acting upon our own best principles.

There are two central solutions to akrasia, located in two unexpected quarters: art and ritual. The real purpose of art (which includes novels, films and songs as well as photos, paintings and works of design and architecture) is to give sensuous and emotional lustre to a range of ideas that are most important to us, but that are also most under threat in the conditions of everyday life. Art shouldn't be a matter of introducing us to, or challenging us with, a stream of new ideas so much as about lending the good ideas we already have compelling forms – so that they can more readily weigh upon our behaviour. A euphoric song should activate the reserves of tenderness and sympathy in which we already believe in theory; a novel should move us to the forgiveness in which we are already invested at an intellectual level. Art should help us to feel and then act upon the truths we already know.

Ritual is the second defence we have against akrasia. By ritual, we mean the structured, often highly seductive or aesthetic, repetition of a thought or an action, with a view to making it at once convincing and habitual. Ritual rejects the notion that it can ever be sufficient to teach anything important once – an optimistic delusion by which the modern education system has been fatefully marked. Once might be enough to get us to admit an idea is right, but is nothing like enough to convince us it should be acted upon. Our brains are leaky, and, under pressure of any kind, readily revert to customary patterns of thought and feeling. Ritual trains our cognitive muscles; it makes a sequence of appointments in our diaries to refresh our acquaintance with our most important ideas.

Our current culture tends to see ritual mainly as an antiquated infringement of individual freedom; a bossy command to turn our thoughts in particular directions at specific times. But the defenders of ritual would see it another way: we aren't being told to think of something we don't agree with; we are being returned with grace to what we always believed in at heart. We are being tugged by a collective force back to a more loyal and authentic version of ourselves.

The greatest human institutions that have tried to address the problem of akrasia have been religions. Religions have wanted to do something much more serious than simply promote abstract ideas: they have wanted to get people to behave in line with those ideas, which is a very different thing. They didn't just want people to think that kindness or forgiveness were nice (which we generally do already); they wanted us to be kind or forgiving most days of the year. They invented a host of ingenious mechanisms for mobilising the will, which is why, across much of the world, the finest art and buildings, the most seductive music, the most impressive and moving rituals have all been religious. Religion is a vast machine for addressing the problem of akrasia.

This has presented a conundrum for a more secular era. Bad secularisation has lumped together religious superstition and religion's anti-akrasia strategies. It has rejected both the supernatural ideas of the faiths and their wise attitude to the motivational roles of art and ritual.

A more discerning form of secularisation makes a major distinction between (on the one hand) religion as a set of speculative claims about God and the afterlife and (on the other hand) the always valid ambition to improve our social and psychological lives by combating our notoriously weak wills.

The challenge for the secular world is now to redevelop its own versions of purposeful art and ritual so that we will cease so regularly to ignore our real commitments and might henceforth not only believe wise things but also, on a day-to-day basis, have a slightly higher chance of enacting wisdom in our lives.

See also: Art, The Purpose of; Art and News; Art for Art's Sake; Censorship; Culture Can Replace Scripture; Envy of the Future; Memento Mori; Pop Music; Ritual; Secularisation; Seduction; Sublime, The; Wisdom.

¶ Androcles and the Lion

A traditional fable tells of a lion prowling villages at night, roaring horribly. Everyone is terrified, so they want to kill the beast to feel a bit safer. One day, in the nearby hills, a shepherd called Androcles gets caught in a sudden storm and seeks shelter in a cave – where the lion has made his home. The terrified shepherd imagines he's about to be ripped to pieces. Then he notices there's a thorn in the lion's paw: the creature is in agony and his terrible roars are his way of trying to express his pain. The shepherd takes a risk: he goes up and removes the thorn. The lion stops roaring, becomes gentle, licks the shepherd's hand and they become friends.

In the fable, the 'lion' represents someone who frightens us. We assume they are determined to destroy us. But the story suggests an alternative explanation: the frightening person is suffering (psychologically rather than physically). It is their pain that drives them to behave in ways that distress and scare us. If we can be brave enough to notice, acknowledge and in some very tender manner address their suffering, we start to take away the cause of their aggression.

The French philosopher Émile-Auguste Chartier (known as Alain) was said to be the finest teacher in France in the first half of the 20th century. He developed a formula for calming down himself and his pupils in the face of irritating people. 'Never say that people are evil,' he wrote; 'You just need to look for the pin.'

What he meant was: look for the source of the agony that drives a person to behave in appalling ways. The calming thought is to imagine that they are suffering off-stage, in some area we cannot see. To be mature is to learn to imagine this zone of pain, despite the lack of available evidence. They may not look as if they were maddened by an inner psychological ailment: they may look aggressive or full of themselves. But the 'pin' simply must be there – or they would not be causing us harm.

See also: Charity of Interpretation; Nastiness; Other-as-Child.

¶ Anger

We start to reduce the danger of anger through the insight that not everything that makes us sad makes us angry. We may be irritated that it is raining, but we are unlikely ever to respond to a shower by screaming. We aren't overwhelmed by anger whenever we are frustrated; we are sent into a rage only when we first allowed ourselves to believe in a hopeful scenario that was then dashed suddenly and apparently without warning. Our greatest furies spring from unfortunate events that we had not factored into our vision of reality.

We typically think of anger as a dark and pessimistic state of mind. But behind anger lies a surprising emotion: optimism. Beneath their ranting, the angry are possessed of some recklessly optimistic notions of how life might go. They are not merely in a destructive fury; they are in the grip of hope.

The person who shouts every time they encounter a traffic jam betrays a faith, at once touching and demented, that roads must always be traffic-free. The person who loses their temper with every new employee or partner evinces a curious belief that perfection is an option for the human animal.

Serenity therefore begins with pessimism. We must learn to disappoint ourselves at leisure before the world ever has a chance to slap us by surprise at a time of its own choosing. The angry must learn to check their fury via a systematic, patient surrender of their more fervent hopes. They need to be carefully inducted into the darkest realities of life, to the stupidities of others, to the ineluctable failings of technology, to the necessary flaws of infrastructure. They should start each day with a short yet thorough premeditation on the many humiliations and insults to which the coming hours risk subjecting them.

One of the goals of civilisation is to instruct us in how to be sad rather than angry. Sadness may not sound very appealing, but in this context it carries a huge advantage. It allows us to detach our emotional energies from fruitless fury around things that (however bad) we cannot change and that are the fault of no-one in particular and – after a period of mourning – to refocus our efforts in places where our few remaining hopes and expectations have a realistic chance of success.

See also: Pessimism; Premeditation; Resilience.

¶ Animals

Animals don't set out to teach us anything, but we have a lot to learn from our interactions with them nevertheless.

Imagine that we come back from work unusually late. It's been a tricky day: a threatened resignation, an enraged supplier, a lost document, two delayed trains … But none of the mayhem is of any concern to one friend waiting by the door, uncomplicatedly pleased to see us: Pippi, a two-year-old border terrier with an appetite for catching a deflated football in her jaws. She wants to play in the usual way, even if it's past nine o'clock now, with us in the chair and her sliding around the kitchen, and, unexpectedly, so do we. We're not offended by her lack of overall interest in us; it's at the root of our delight. Here, at last, is someone indifferent to almost everything about us except for our dexterity at ball-throwing; someone who doesn't care about the Brussels meeting, who will forgive us for not warning the finance department in time about the tax rebates and for whom the Lisbon conference is beyond imagining.

One of the most consoling aspects of animals – whether a dog, sheep, lizard or beetle – is that their priorities have nothing to do with our own perilous and tortured agendas. They are redemptively unconcerned with everything we are and want. They implicitly mock our self-importance and absorption and so return us to a fairer, more modest, sense of our role on the planet.

A sheep doesn't know about our feelings of jealousy; it has no interest in our humiliation and bitterness around a colleague; it has never sent an email. On a walk in the hills, it simply ambles towards the path we're on and looks curiously at us, then takes a lazy mouthful of grass, chewing from the side of its mouth as though it were gum. One of its companions approaches and sits next to it, wool to wool; for a second, they exchange what appears to be a knowing, mildly amused, glance.

Ducks nibble at the weeds, waddle down to the water and paddle about in circles without any interest in which century it happens to be from a human point of view; they've never heard of the economy; they don't know what country they live in; they don't have new ideas or regret what happened yesterday. They don't care about the career hurdles or relationship status of the person who sprinkles a few breadcrumbs near them.

Time around animals invites us into a world in which most of the things that obsess us have no significance. It corrects our characteristic over-investment in matters that make only a limited contribution to the essential task of existence: to be kind, to make the most of our talents, to love and to appreciate.

See also: Nature; Sublime, The

¶ Anxiety

Anxiety is not a sign of sickness, a weakness of the mind or an error to which we should always locate a medical solution. It is mostly a reasonable and sensitive response to the genuine strangeness, terror, uncertainty and riskiness of existence.

Anxiety is our fundamental state for well-founded reasons: because we are intensely vulnerable physical beings, a complicated network of fragile organs all biding their time before letting us down catastrophically at a moment of their own choosing. Because we have insufficient information upon which to make most major life decisions. Because we can imagine so much more than we have, and live in ambitious mediatised societies where envy and restlessness are constant. Because we are the descendants of the great worriers of the species, the others having been trampled and torn apart by wild animals, and because we still carry in our DNA – into the calm of the suburbs – the terrors of the savannah. Because the progress of our careers and of our finances plays out within the tough-minded, competitive, destructive, random workings of an uncontained economic engine. Because we rely for our self-esteem and sense of comfort on the love of people we cannot control and whose needs and hopes will never align seamlessly with our own.

All of which is not to say that there aren't better and worse ways to approach our condition. The single most important move is acceptance. There is no need to be anxious that we are anxious on top of everything else. The mood is no sign that our lives have gone wrong; merely that we are alive. We should also be more careful when pursuing things we imagine will spare us anxiety. We can head to them by all means, but for other reasons than fantasies of calm – and with a little less vigour and a little more scepticism. We will still be anxious when we finally have the house, the love affair and the right income.

We should spare ourselves the burden of loneliness. We are far from the only ones with this problem. Everyone is more anxious than they are inclined to tell us. Even the tycoon and the couple in love are suffering. We have collectively failed to admit to ourselves how much we panic.

We must learn to laugh about our anxieties – laughter being the exuberant expression of relief when a hitherto private agony is given a well-crafted social formulation in a joke. We must suffer alone. But we can at least hold out our arms to our similarly tortured, fractured, and above all else, anxious neighbours, as if to say, in the kindest way possible: 'I know…'

Anxiety deserves greater dignity. It is not a sign of degeneracy. It is a kind of masterpiece of insight: a justifiable expression of our mysterious participation in a disordered, uncertain world.

See also: Normality; Pessimism.

¶ Anxious Attachment

Anxious attachment is a pattern of relating to lovers whereby, when difficulty arises, we grow officious, procedural and controlling over small matters of domestic routine.

We feel our partners are escaping us emotionally, but rather than admitting our sense of loss, we respond by trying to pin them down administratively. We get unduly cross that they are eight minutes late; we chastise them for not having done certain chores; we ask them strictly if they've completed a task they had only vaguely agreed to undertake. All this rather than admit the truth: 'I'm worried that I don't matter to you...'

We can't (we believe) force our partner to be generous and warm. We can't force them to want us, even if we haven't asked them to. So we try to control them practically. The goal isn't really to be in charge all the time; it's just that we can't admit to our terror at how much we need them. A tragic cycle then unfolds. We become shrill and unpleasant. To the other person, it feels like we can't possibly love them anymore. The truth is that we do: we just fear rather too much that they don't love us. As a final recourse, we may ward off our vulnerability by denigrating the person who eludes us. We pick up on their weaknesses and complain about their extensive practical shortcomings. Anything rather than ask the question that disturbs us so much: does this person love me? If this harsh, graceless, anxious behaviour could be understood for what it truly is, it would be revealed not as a rejection, but as a strangely distorted, yet very real and very touching, plea for tenderness.

See also: Avoidant Attachment; Closeness.

¶ Appreciation

At the centre of our societies is a hugely inventive force dedicated to nudging us towards a heightened appreciation of certain aspects of the world. With enormous skill, it throws into relief the very best sides of particular places and objects. It uses wordsmiths and image-makers of near-genius, who create deeply inspiring and beguiling associations – and it positions works close to our eyelines at most moments of the day.

Advertising is the most compelling agent of mass appreciation the world has ever known. It hones our sensitivity to the elegant styling of a car bonnet or to the niceties of design around training shoes; we become acutely receptive to the personalities of handbags or sunglasses. Because advertising is ubiquitous, it can be easy to forget that only a limited range of things ever get advertised; only a limited range of products can support the budgets for prominent advertising campaigns.

Christen Købke, *Morning Light*, 1836.
This Danish artist brought touching awareness to an often-underappreciated subject:
cloudy skies.

One of the tasks of art is to teach us appreciation of many other important things. In the 1830s, the Danish artist Christen Købke did a lot of advertising for the sky, especially just before or after a rain shower.

His 'product' was, in effect, rain clouds, whose market share of love he felt was disappointing, like a delicious biscuit that hadn't yet found its market. Obviously, he wasn't trying to get us to buy a cloud. But, just like an advertiser, he wanted us to be much more sensitive than we normally are to the charms of grey skies; how they go so nicely with small patches of sunlight; how they enhance a quiet moment in a busy day; how they can make the ordinary feel special. Under his guidance, we are sensitised to different kinds of cloud: some are attractively independent, some fluffy and light, others massy and assertive.

Other works of art might advertise kindness or melancholy; the loveliness of trees or night-time walks; going to bed early, or making a heartfelt apology.

Art is advertising for the things that really matter, but that aren't usually for sale.

See also: Art, The Purpose of; Kintsugi; Rock Appreciation; Ugliness; Water Towers.

¶ Architecture

In an odd but quietly very important way, works of architecture 'speak' to us. Some buildings, streets and even whole cities seem to speak of chaos, aggression or military pride; others seem to whisper to us of calm or graceful dignity, generosity or gentleness.

However, a dominant strand of modern opinion doesn't think it matters much what our buildings speak to us about. It is deemed pretentious or over-sensitive to suppose that something as external as a building could have much effect on our mood. We'd rather see ourselves as able to generate our psychological states independently of the colour, shape and texture of walls.

And yet a more modest, permeable idea of who we are would accept with good grace that we remain vulnerable to the voices of the largest, most public objects in our environment. Our inner states are open to influence and we may be as harmed by architectural ugliness as we are by moral evil. Our spirits can be decisively sunk by a grid of city streets designed without any talent or care.

In modern commercial society, buildings are seen largely in terms of finance, cost and return on capital. Politicians impose some restraints on developers. There are frequently a few rules about height and environmental performance. But the full range of the kinds of damage that ugly buildings create for us has not been recognised or granted political expression. There is nothing unusual in this. Many forms of public harm can be real yet ignored; it took many decades for the pollution of rivers to be interpreted as a real threat to the public good.

If we better understood the impact that ugly architecture has on our lives, its power to sap our spirits and assist our worst selves, we would surely legislate against it. But as yet, no politician who announced an intention to make the built environment more beautiful would prosper – or even be deemed sane.

In the Utopia, architecture would more fairly be interpreted as a branch of mental health, with a crucial role to play in public contentment. And bad design would be interpreted as a crime to the health of the collective spirit.

See also: Art, The Purpose of; Fashion; Home; Monasteries.

¶ Art, The Purpose of

The idea that art might not have a purpose is a relatively new one, emerging only in France in the middle of the 19th century. For the rest of history, in every established civilisation, it has seemed obvious that art has certain specific and important tasks to perform.

To summarise the objectives, the role of art has been: to give us a more accurate picture of the inner lives of other people; to show us what 'normal' really means and thus assuage our loneliness and shyness; to embolden the confession of our vulnerabilities by giving us greater confidence that others will understand; to console us in our sorrows; to draw our attention to pleasures we might otherwise overlook; to make important but not initially alluring ideas seductive and glamorous, so that we can more easily embrace them; to enlarge our sympathies for people who are not outwardly successful – not by making us feel guilty but by showing us what is genuinely admirable and attractive about them; and to take an ice pick to the frozen surface of our being and reconnect us with the deeper emotions on which our friendships, relationships and ambitions depend.

The key thing about art was identified by the Ancient Roman poet Horace: poetry (and art in general) should both 'delight and instruct'. The combination is vital: there is so much in which we need to be instructed, but we will not learn unless we are delighted. The essential task of artists is to find the way to get round our boredom and our defences and entice us to pay serious attention to those ideas we need to keep at the front of our minds in order to live and die well.

See also: Akrasia; Appreciation; Architecture; Art and News; Art for Art's Sake; Artistic Rebalancing; Artistic Sympathy; Culture Can Replace Scripture; Inner Voices; Memento Mori; Music; Normality; Rock Appreciation; Sane Insanity; Seduction; Water Towers.

¶ Art and News

News organisations are overwhelmingly focused on gathering information – assuming that if the information is significant, it will immediately go deep into our hearts and minds. But in truth, facts are rarely enough. We too often get bored and turn away when the facts, however important they might be, are heaped in front of us in a dry or confrontational way. In order to matter to us, facts have to be shaped so that they can enter our imaginations. To do justice to the material it handles every day, news needs to become a little more like art.

A standard response on the part of frustrated news organisations is to blame us, the audience, for not caring enough. The reason we don't care about important things must be that we're stupid or selfish. The inclination is then to nag, to make us feel guilty for, and ashamed of, our indifference. This approach might work for a small number of people, but is usually ineffective. We simply stop listening. We just don't care about yet another victim, refugee or instance of tyranny.

But another, kinder and more realistic, way of thinking about our indifference is to see it as the consequence of a failure of art. There is no such thing as a boring story, only a story told in a boring way. Pretty much any sequence of events could be made compelling in the hands of a talented artist.

An instance of the power of art in relation to the news can be found in a strange historical episode. During the 1820s, the British public became obsessed with the Greek War of Independence, during which Greece broke away from the Ottoman Empire after Britain offered decisive material assistance to the rebels. This was surprising because there was no obvious interest for Britain in the move. The reason for the involvement was more or less entirely due to the impassioned support and advocacy of the most famous writer of the era: the poet Lord Byron. In one poem he wrote:

The mountains look on Marathon –
And Marathon looks on the sea;
And musing there an hour alone,
I dreamed that Greece might still be free.

Byron didn't pile up statistics or argue a complex political case. He didn't scold. He painted an emotional picture. The entire educated population of England knew of the ancient battle of Marathon and of the famous run that brought news of victory to Athens. Byron was conveying a sense of the grandeur of the current struggle and making people in Hampshire and Sussex feel that events unfolding in the Peloponnese mattered to them as much as something in their own village. Byron was not above a few salacious and sentimental moves: he wrote of how attractive Greek women were and lamented that, unless the War of Independence was won, 'such breasts must suckle slaves'.

Art seduces: it can be defined as the skill of making an idea immediately powerful via an appeal to the senses. This isn't a climbdown; it is a wise recognition of how our minds function. The newsrooms of the Utopia would be largely staffed by artists, so that the most important messages could be made to lodge properly and powerfully in our erratic and distracted minds.

See also: Akrasia; Art, The Purpose of; Changing the World; News; Seduction

¶ Art for Art's Sake

In answer to the question of what art might be for, the established reply is to point out rather scornfully that it isn't for anything. As a famous saying goes, art is for art's sake.

The expression dates back to mid-19th-century France, an era of nascent industrialisation and scientific progress that grew highly concerned with the notion of 'usefulness'. Those who wished to attack art and its values asked what it really ever achieved, and therefore whether it still deserved the respect it had traditionally enjoyed. Could a painting build a railway? Could a poem bake bread? Might a sculpture transport one across an ocean? And given that they obviously couldn't, was this not proof of the underlying pretension and superfluity of art?

In reaction to such assaults, the artistic community grew brittle and defiant; it embraced the intended criticism but turned it into a point of pride: art, it said, is too lofty and important to be merely useful. Its glory must lie somewhere else, in being above petty concerns, in its sheer wondrous uselessness. The more the world grew shrill in its questioning and materialistic in its values, the more artists turned away angrily and defensively from the very idea of purpose.

In cultural circles, it became taboo to wonder too loudly what a given poem or painting might be for. To ask what good might come of a certain piece of music or a play was taken as a sign of unforgivable Philistinism. Art became a cult of inutility, apparently best loved and most accomplished when it was ethereally devoid of purpose.

But this was a tragic misunderstanding of what artists can do for us. Baking bread, building railways or crossing oceans cover only a fraction of what deserves to be counted as useful. To lead good lives, we need not merely lightbulbs and telephone lines, chemicals and stock exchanges; we also need to be consoled in our griefs, guided towards wisdom, opened up to self-knowledge, calmed in our anxieties, given new hope and introduced to wider horizons – all tasks for which the practical tool known as art is eminently suited. Only under a desperately narrow vision of usefulness could art ever be dismissed as useless.

Unfortunately, though, the notion of art for art's sake has maintained a powerful presence in modern culture – especially in the artist community itself. In the top universities, among leading cultural critics, in the great museums, it remains taboo to speak of purpose, or to ask that art should help us with our confusions, melancholy and loneliness.

To do justice to art, we should recover the traditional, pre-19th-century assessment of its role: the sense that it is an overwhelmingly practical medium designed to help us live and die well. Art is there to guide, console, provide balance and perspective, to calm and reassure us, to offer us more accurate ideas about the inner lives of others and to present important concepts in seductive and sensuous clothing, in order to combat our forgetfulness and coldness of heart.

The phrase 'art for art's sake' was born to defend art from unfair attack, but it ended up fatefully weakening it, blinding us to its real role in society. The salvation of art does not lie in thinking of it as useless, we can now see, but in remembering and rehearsing the very serious reasons for its overwhelming utility within the span of every good life.

See also: Akrasia; Art, The Purpose of; Artistic Rebalancing; Philosophy; Self-Help Books; Tragedy.

¶ Artistic Consolation

We live in what is often a vibrantly optimistic, jollying culture that subtly stigmatises feelings of sorrow. But around certain works of art we're invited to a very different view of darkness. These art works remember how much of life deserves solemn and mournful states. The private agonies of our souls have been the subjects of art down the ages: unhappy love, discrimination, anxiety, sexual humiliation, rivalry, regret, shame, isolation and frustrated longing are the core of the artistic canon.

The great sad works do not cheer us up by directing our thoughts towards happy scenes. They do so via a more sombre but effective route: they show us that we are not alone in our griefs.

Standing as a record of the tears of humanity, art lends legitimacy to despair and replays our miseries back to us with dignity, shorn of many of their haphazard or trivial particulars. 'A book [though the same could be said of any art form] must be the axe for the frozen sea inside us,' proposed Kafka; in other words, an art work is a tool to help release us from our numbness, to allow us to shed tears and to provide occasions for catharsis in areas where we have for too long been damagingly brave.

See also: Consolation; Eudaimonia; Jolliness.

¶ Artistic Philanthropy

There is a large and prominent tradition of philanthropy that wishes to serve civilised values and seeks to promote them via sometimes enormous donations to the arts. A portion of the surplus wealth created in one area (oil, supermarkets, construction, the media) is deposited in another: public art galleries. The paintings and sculpture on display often murmur quietly about the deepest and loveliest things: compassion for the secret sorrows of existence, the splendour of nature, harmony, the honour of sacrifice, the strange glory of a sunflower, the sweet moodiness of dusk. The hope is that, by a circuitous route, these values will become – even if only a little – more powerful in reality. In the ideal scenario, they will radiate out from the gallery and shape the way we lead our lives.

Yet the money that paid for them may have been accumulated under a very different vision of life: workers were paid the least possible amounts; only the responsibilities enforced by law were embraced; governments were lobbied to reduce consumer and environmental protection; quality was reduced as low as the market would allow; debts were paid slowly but creditors were hounded. Oddly, in their business, the artistic philanthropist had the opportunity to make real – on a large scale – the qualities they subsequently sought to honour in their gifts. Yet very often they did not.

It would be better to repatriate the ambition and for the capitalists to be themselves the agents of the virtues they admire in the arts. The cost (in terms of cash) might be approximately the same. Their businesses might be a little less profitable year by year and they might not feel they had enough left over to lavish on the arts. But it would be no loss, for instead of hanging reticently on a wall, those values so ably captured in art – of friendship, love, wisdom and beauty – would be enacted day to day in the boardroom and the canteen, the distribution centre and the factory – in other words, in the vastly more consequential realm of commerce itself.

See also: Good Business.

¶ Artistic Rebalancing

Few of us are entirely well 'balanced'. Our psychological histories, relationships and working routines mean that many of our emotions incline a little too much in one direction or another.

Fortunately, this is an issue that culture is well placed to help us with, for works of art can put us powerfully in touch with concentrated doses of our missing dispositions, and thereby restore a measure of equilibrium to our listing inner selves.

Imagine that we have fallen into a way of life that suffers from too much intensity, stimulation and distraction. Work is frantic across three continents. The inbox is clogged with two hundred messages every hour. There is hardly time to reflect

John Pawson, *The Life House,* 2016.
A minimalist interior offers quiet beauty to balance out over-stimulation.

on anything once the day starts. This explains why we might be powerfully drawn to a minimalist interior, where things appear calm, logical and reduced to their essence. This is our true home, from which our way of life has exiled us.

But because we are not all missing the same things, the kinds of art that have a capacity to rebalance us, and therefore arouse enthusiasm in us, will differ markedly. Imagine we happen to be a bureaucrat in one of the sleepier branches of the Norwegian civil service based in the idyllic though rather quiet town of Trondheim near the Arctic Circle. Our days run like clockwork. We are always home by 5.15pm and do the crossword before bed. The last thing we may be attracted to is a pristinely ordered home by John Pawson. We might be drawn instead to Flamenco music, the paintings of Frida Kahlo and the architecture of Mexico's Catedral de Santa Prisca – varieties of art to restore life to our slumbering souls.

Façade of the Catedral de Santa Prisca y San Sebastian, Taxco, Mexico,
constructed 1751–1758.
Art to rebalance an over-quiet soul.

Edmund Blair Leighton, *The End of the Song*, 1902.
Art to rebalance oneself after too many railways, factories and readings of Darwin.

Jacques-Louis David, *The Oath of the Horatii*, 1784.
Art to rebalance oneself after overindulgence in mistresses, gold and parties.

Whole nations can manifest longings for balance and will use art to help them achieve it. After too much aristocratic decadence, many in late 18th-century France felt the need to get back in touch with marshal solemnity and spartan simplicity and so found refuge in the pared-down works of Jacques-Louis David.

By the later part of the 19th century in England, the materialism, scientific obsession and capitalist rationality of the age drove many to long for more faithful, mystical days, and so to locate 'beauty' in the images inspired by the literature and history of the Middle Ages.

What we call 'beautiful' is any work of art that supplies a missing dose of a much-needed psychological component, and we dismiss as 'ugly' one that forces on us moods or motifs by which we feel threatened or are already overwhelmed. Our contact with art holds out the promise of inner wholeness.

See also: Art, The Purpose of; Art for Art's Sake; Music.

¶ Artistic Sympathy

One of the most troubling aspects of our world is that it contains such enormous disparities in income. At various times, there have been concerted attempts to correct the injustice. Inspired by Marxism, Communist governments forcibly seized private wealth and Socialist governments have repeatedly tried imposing punitive taxes on rich companies and individuals. There have also been attempts to reform the education system, to create positive discrimination in the workplace and to seize the estates of the wealthiest members of society at their deaths.

But the problem of inequality has not gone away, and is unlikely to be solved at any point soon, let alone in the short timeframe that is relevant to any of us, for a range of stubbornly embedded, partly logical, partly absurd reasons.

However, there is one important move we can make that could reduce some of the sting of inequality. For this, we need to begin by asking what might sound like an offensively obvious question: why is financial inequality a problem?

There are two very different answers. One kind of harm is material: not being able to get a decent house, quality healthcare, a proper education and a hopeful future for one's children. But there is also a psychological reason why inequality proves so problematic: because poverty is intricately bound up with humiliation and lack of respect. The punishment of poverty is not limited to money; it extends to the suffering that attends a lack of status, a constant low-level sense that who one is and what one does is of no interest to a world that is punitively unequal in its distribution of honour as well as cash. Poverty not only induces financial harm, but also damages mental health as well.

Historically, the bulk of political effort has been directed at the first material problem, yet there is also an important move we can make around the psychological issue.

The sketch of the solution to the gap between income and respect lies in a slightly unexpected place: hanging in a top-floor gallery of London's Wallace Collection in Manchester Square is a small painting called *The Lacemaker,* by the little-known German artist Caspar Netscher, who painted it in 1662.

The artist has caught the woman making lace at a moment of intense concentration on a difficult task. We can feel the effort she is making and can imagine the skill and intelligence she is devoting to her work. At the time the painting was created, lace was highly prized. But because many people knew how to make it, the economic law of supply and demand meant that the reward for exquisite craftsmanship was tiny. Lacemakers were among the poorest in society. Were the artist working today, his portrait would have been equivalent to making a short film about office cleaners or fruit pickers. It would have been evident to all the painting's viewers that the lacemaker

Caspar Netscher, *The Lacemaker*, 1662.
This beautiful painting lends grace and dignity to the otherwise humble lacemaker.

was someone who ordinarily had no respect at all; this was a vision of the lowest of the low.

However, Netscher directed an extraordinary amount of what one might call artistic sympathy towards his sitter. Through his eyes and artistry, she is no longer a nobody. She has grown into an individual, full of her own thoughts, sensitive, serious, complicated, devoted; entirely deserving of tenderness and consideration. The artist has transformed how we might look at a lacemaker.

Netscher isn't sternly saying that we should have respect for the low-paid; we hear this often enough and the lesson rarely sinks in. He is not trying to use guilt, which is rarely an effective tactic. He's getting us to feel respect for his worker rather than just know it might be her due. His picture isn't nagging, grim or forbidding; it is a seductive, delightful mechanism for teaching us a very unfamiliar but critically important supra-political emotion.

If lots of people saw the lacemaker in the way the artist did, took the lesson properly to heart and applied it widely and imaginatively at every moment of their lives, it is no exaggeration to say that the psychological burden of poverty would be lifted substantially. The fate of lacemakers, but also warehouse attendants, delivery workers, labourers and those presently dehumanised under the vast category we know as 'immigrants' would be significantly improved. Greater sympathy would not be a replacement for political action; it would be its precondition – the sentiment upon which a material change in the lives of the victims of inequality would be founded.

An artist like Netscher isn't changing how much the low-paid earn; he is changing how the low-paid are judged. This is not an unimportant piece of progress. Netscher was living in an age in which only a very few people might ever see a picture – and of course he was concentrating only on the then current face of poverty. But the process he undertook remains profoundly relevant.

Ideally today, our culture would pursue the very same project but on a vastly enlarged scale, enticing us via our most successful, popular and widespread art forms to a grand political revolution in feeling, upon which an eventual, firmly based revolution in economic distribution would arise.

See also: Art, The Purpose of; Nagging; Suicide; Tragedy; Universal Love.

¶ Avoidant Attachment

Avoidant attachment is a pattern of relating to lovers whereby, when difficulty arises, we grow cold and distant and deny our need for anyone. We desperately want to be reassured, but feel so anxious that we may be unwanted that we disguise our need behind a façade of indifference. At the precise moment when we want to be close, we say we're busy, we pretend our thoughts are elsewhere, we get sarcastic and dry; we imply that a need for reassurance would be the last thing on our minds. We might even have an affair, the ultimate face-saving attempt to be distant – and often a perverse attempt to assert that we don't require a partner's love (which we have been too reserved to ask for).

See also: Anxious Attachment; Closeness.

¶ Bad Taste

In matters of design and decoration, it has grown taboo to accuse anyone of having 'bad taste'. The official story is that no one knows what good or bad taste might be and that every taste must be of equal validity.

Yet this appears both untrue to experience and lacking in ambition. To make progress, we should begin by considering the psychological mechanisms that govern the business of taste. We need to consider the theory of artistic rebalancing. We are all somewhat unbalanced inside and grow attracted to artistic styles that promise to compensate us for, or 'correct', the things we lack within. This explains why people who feel chaotic, undisciplined and cluttered inside are liable to be drawn to interiors that are serene, pure and poised. Equally, people who are exposed to, and oppressed by, the hurried tempo of modern life are often drawn to styles that speak of the rustic and the natural.

What singles out 'bad taste' is merely that the desire for compensation has grown particularly acute because the deprivation has been correspondingly intense. Those who have experienced crushing poverty will, if the opportunity arises, often adopt a gaudy style derived from the most gilded aspects of the palace of Versailles. Those whose lives are excessively harsh may favour garden gnomes, enormous and brightly coloured stuffed toys and sentimental trinkets.

In every instance of bad taste, we find an over-eager embracing of a good quality – sweetness, freedom, fun or prosperity – that is, or once was, in very short supply in the owner's life. Bad taste can appal, but once one understands its origins, sympathy is a more appropriate response.

What is 'bad' in bad taste is not the person, but the prior difficulty for which they are seeking to compensate through their décor. There is no point in mocking or offering lectures about art history. The problem isn't a lack of information. It is a trauma created by a badly broken and unbalanced world. Therefore, the solution to bad taste is, in the broad sense, political. Good taste comes about when people feel appreciated, when there's enough to go around and when there's an economy that doesn't routinely humiliate and abase its members. To make good taste more widespread, what matters above all are efforts to diminish the desperate lives in which lapses of taste invariably have their origins.

See also: Artistic Rebalancing; Charity of Interpretation; Universal Love.

¶ Being 'Good'

We tend to assume that all is well with good children. They don't pose immediate problems; they keep their bedroom tidy, do their homework on time and are willing to help with the washing up. But the very real secret sorrows – and future difficulties – of the good child are tied to the fact that they behave in this way not out of choice, but because they feel under irresistible pressure to do so. They are trying to cope with adults who project the idea that only the ideally compliant child is truly loveable.

As a result, the good child becomes an expert at pleasing their audience, while their real thoughts and feelings stay buried. Eventually, under pressure, these good children may manifest some disturbing symptoms: secret sulphurous bitterness, sudden outbursts of rage and very harsh views of their own imperfections.

The good person typically has particular problems around sex. As a child, they may have been praised for being pure and innocent. As an adult the most exciting parts of their own sexuality strike them as perverse, disgusting and deeply at odds with who they are meant to be. As an adult, the good child is likely to have problems at work as well. They feel too strong a need to follow the rules, never make trouble or annoy anyone. But almost everything that is interesting or worth doing will meet with a degree of opposition and will seriously irritate some people. The good child is condemned to career mediocrity and sterile people-pleasing.

The desire to be good is one of the loveliest things in the world, but in order to have a genuinely good life, we may sometimes need to be (by the standards of the good child) fruitfully and bravely bad.

See also: Duty Trap, The; Love as Generosity; Splitting and Integration.

¶ Better Porn

The idea of good porn can seem paradoxical. Many of us are used to thinking of all porn as 'bad'. Yet when people eat badly, we don't try to stop them eating at all. We hope to improve their diet. The aim isn't to abolish food just because some food is terrible. We want good food to be more widely and easily available. The same move could apply to online sex sites. We can't abolish porn, so the goal is to get good pornography.

Better porn isn't even more thrilling or exciting. It is 'better' in the sense of being less at odds with the rest of our lives. It isn't merely about sex, but also about other things we care about, like self-understanding, kindness, intelligence and good relationships. Unfortunately, we have left porn largely in the hands of people who don't seem to be interested in anything much apart from sex. Better porn would reconnect sexuality with other parts of our lives.

We shouldn't be negative about porn just because of how most of it seems today. In 1800, many people offering medical services were quacks. They didn't know what they were doing. There was a hunger for remedies, however misguided. So 'being a doctor' was nothing like the respectable career choice it is today. What changed was the realisation that we needed really serious, thoughtful and honourable people to go into the medical field. Health was too important to be left to self-appointed peddlers of fanciful potions.

We are hugely aware of the things that can go wrong around porn in the internet age. But the longing for sexual stimulation isn't going to go away. Given how vast the demand is, and how crucial the role of sexuality is in life, it is tragic that comparatively so little talent, wisdom, intelligence, maturity and aesthetic imagination has been directed to it. We've rightly come to fear bad porn because it damages so many lives. Good porn could help us deal a little better with the complex, tricky fact of being at the same time highly sexual and highly reasonable beings.

(The School of Life has developed its own porn site, available at: www.pornastherapy.com).

See also: Sexual Liberation.

¶ Bounded Work

The wider world will always be a mess. But around work, we can sometimes have a radically different kind of experience: we get on top of a problem and finally resolve it. We bring order to chaos in a way that we rarely can in other areas of life.

The Zen Buddhist monks of medieval Japan had an intuitive understanding of this kind of benefit to work. In order to achieve peace of mind, they recommended that members of a monastery regularly rake the gravel of their intricately plotted and bounded temple gardens around Kyoto. Within the confines of a large courtyard space, the monks could bring total coherence and beauty to fruition. It wasn't completely easy. The monks loved to make ambitious patterns of swirls and circles. The lines were often on a very small scale; they might inadvertently tread on a bit they'd already done; they might struggle to keep the rake going at just the right angle. It was sometimes maddening, especially when it was autumn and there were leaves everywhere. But it could, eventually, all be put right. With time and a bit of careful correction and a well-trained hand, they could get everything just as it should be. The problems were real, but they were bounded – and they could be solved.

We are not wrong to love perfection, but it brings us a lot of pain. At its best, our work offers us a patch of gravel that we can rake, a bounded space we can make ideally tidy and via which we can fulfil our powerful inner need for order and control, so often thwarted in a wider world beset by defiant unruliness.

In a small but real way, through our work, we are clearing and cultivating a tiny portion of a wild surrounding forest and turning it into a harmonious, comprehensible garden.

See also: Flowers; Quiet Life, The.

¶ Censorship

Censorship is one of the most frightening of all political restrictions, associated with tyranny, the banning of legitimate criticism, state-sanctioned abuse and dictatorship.

These are hugely legitimate concerns. However, they can make it harder for us to recognise a few ways in which certain kinds of censorship may be genuinely helpful to us and align with our best interests.

Good censorship starts from an admission that we suffer from a congenital weakness of the will (akrasia). There is so much we would like to do, eat, say and be, but we are horribly prone to be pulled towards less admirable patterns of behaviour. We give in to passing desires, we are defenceless before certain passions, and we end up acting in ways we profoundly regret. This isn't a severe judgement about the failings of other people; it's a frank confession of our own private inadequacies.

Good censorship takes our weaknesses seriously and wants to help us with them. It isn't about a bossy instinct to clamp down on the rest of society; it's the realisation that a

C

well-calibrated dose of censorship might be of genuine assistance in our attempts to lead good lives. We may willingly give up the keys to someone else, surrendering to external authority in order to nurture our own best but fragile instincts.

We might, for example, end up profoundly grateful to live in a society that doesn't make it too easy to eat the wrong things, to spend our money in fitful ways, to exploit other people through our purchases, to develop addictions, or to aggravate our febrile compulsive sides. It isn't so much the authorities who might want this for us; it's we who want it for ourselves. Good censorship limits our freedom to do anything in the name of liberating us to be who we want to become deep down. We may long for a little gently administered censorship to protect our best from our worst selves.

See also: Akrasia; Emotional Scepticism; Faulty Walnut, The; News.

¶ Changing the World

The world needs to be changed in many urgent ways: the great question is how this change might best occur.

The Romantic view is that the world is sick because of a lack of good ideas. Therefore, the most prestigious and urgent move might be to withdraw and write a book or start a think tank, and thereby work out what justice is, solutions for climate change, why relationships don't work, or why there is so much inequality.

Immense prestige has surrounded the gestation of new ideas for helping humanity for the last three hundred years. And yet the world has continued to change a lot less than it should, remaining surprisingly committed to its familiar wicked ways, despite the existence of so many revolutionary and truly wise plans.

This is perhaps because we have missed an insight. The world is not principally in the state it is because we lack good ideas. We know almost everything we could ever need to know about justice, beauty, wisdom, truth and kindness. Our problem isn't a deficit of good ideas; it's a stubborn inability to act upon and correctly implement the many good ideas we already have.

The world is not held together simply by ideas: it is made up of laws, practices, institutions, financial arrangements, businesses and governments. In other words, improvements cannot be made lasting and effective until legions of people start to work together and begin the unglamorous and boring task of wrestling with tangled issues of law, money, long-term mass communication, advocacy and administration.

In the single greatest book of philosophy ever written, *The Republic,* Plato articulated a provocative understanding (gathered from bitter experience) of the limits of intellectuals, when he remarked that the world would never be set right until, in his words, 'philosophers become kings, or kings philosophers'. He was advising that thinkers should stop imagining that ideas alone can ever change reality and urging us to recognise that it is only through the command of institutions – 'kingship', in this context – that we have any chance of exerting a proper influence on the world.

The reason why philosophers have found it so hard to become kings very often comes down to issues of temperament. Those with the good ideas have been bad with money; they have grown tetchy around details; they have not liked to campaign or team up; they have had spiky characters; they didn't like going to the office or sharing a platform. They were wary of popularisation and diffusion: they secretly liked embattled exclusivity. They may even have been rather proud of their inability to read a balance sheet. Such Romantic prejudices have kept the status quo reliably unchanged.

Sole authorship and sporadic individual impassioned action cannot be a logical long-term way to address the complexities of the most significant global issues. Changing the world requires patient and impersonal teamwork: it calls out for the collective efforts of entrepreneurs and product managers, accountants and media strategists, lawyers and activists, members of parliament and social workers. Change takes years: it is made up of many very small victories; it involves compromises at every stage, and it is accompanied by countless humiliating reversals.

It all sounds very un-Romantic – and that's the point. The only way to bring about the change we need is to alter our sense of how change really occurs – away from exclusivity, intellectualism and spontaneity and in the direction of modesty, patience, rigour and collaboration.

See also: Art and News; Classical; Romantic; Seduction; State Broadcasting.

¶ Charity of Interpretation

At its most basic, charity means giving someone something they need but can't get for themselves. Normally this is understood to mean something material; we overwhelmingly associate charity with giving money.

However, at its core, charity goes far beyond finance. It is about the interpretation of motives. It involves seeing that another person's bad behaviour is not a sign of wickedness or sin, but is a result of suffering.

The psychologically charitable feel inwardly 'fortunate' enough to be able to come forward with explanations of others' misdeeds – their impatience or over-ambition, rashness or rage – that take attenuating circumstances into account. They generate a picture of who another person might be that can make them seem more than simply mean or mad.

In financial matters, charity tends always to flow in one direction. The philanthropist may be very generous, but they normally stay rich; they are habitually the giver rather than the recipient. But in our relationships with others more broadly, the need for charity is unlikely ever to end up being one-sided, for we all stand in need of constant generosity of interpretation. We are never far from requiring help in explaining to the world why we are not as awful as we appear.

See also: Androcles and the Lion; Bad Taste; Other-as-Child; Universal Love; Weakness of Strength.

¶ Cheerful Despair

One of philosophy's most established oppositions, depicted in art throughout the centuries, is between two great Greek thinkers, Democritus and Heraclitus. Both men (who lived to a very old age) had a deep knowledge of people and the world, but responded to what they knew in strikingly different ways. Heraclitus could not stop weeping; Democritus could not stop laughing.

Crucially, Democritus laughed not because a privileged position led him to naively misunderstand how bad things could be. His good humour wasn't a version of sentimentality or avoidant optimism. Nor was it simply a random quirk of temperament. Democritus laughed in a very particular and admirable way because he had learnt the subtle art of Cheerful Despair.

The philosopher recommended that we acquaint ourselves with the totality of human experience, with all its failings, follies, self-deception and casual (and not so casual) injustices. The wise person should take care to grow completely at home with the ordinary shambles of existence. They must never be taken by surprise or shocked by how things can be, for they have taken full notice of the facts and so can be embittered by nothing. Betrayal, murder, sexual deviance, corruption – all are already factored in. The wise understand that they are living on a dunghill. When baseness and malice rear their heads, as they will, it is against a backdrop of fully vanquished hope, so there will be no sense of having been unfairly let down and one's credulity betrayed. Democritus was so convinced of the darkness, he no longer had to register it constantly at the front of his mind in order to do it justice. It seemed an entirely obvious, baseline fact about existence.

The laughing Greek could be cheerful, because anything nice, sweet or charming that came his way was immediately experienced as a bonus; a deeply gratifying addition to his original bleak premises. By keeping the dark backdrop of life always in mind, he sharpened his appreciation of whatever stood out against it. He did not have to be on constant high alert for the negative; he had the inner space to listen out for the faintest signals of redemption. The positive was not a feeble echo of dashed hopes; it was a particularly delightful, slightly improbable but noteworthy bucking of the usual and expected tragic trend.

Democritus was known to be fond of parties. He enjoyed wine and drinking. 'A life without festivity is a long road without an inn', he wrote. His occasional frivolities weren't a rejection of his more serious insights and tasks; they were what kept up his spirits so that he could continue to engage with the difficulties of life. Therefore, although they might not have been serious in themselves, they had an extremely serious role to play in the overall economy of his existence. Democritus did not believe that he had to feel constantly sad to prove that he recognised life to be sad. He danced every now and then because of a rightful confidence that he had already done justice, and would always in the future fully do justice, to the sadness of things.

Once we have acquired the skill of Cheerful Despair, a new range of possibilities for pleasure opens itself up to us. We will be amazed and touched when, once in a while, someone seems to understand a few things we mean. We will take note, with some astonishment, that not everyone has plans to murder or hurt others. We will make the most of the constrained but real opportunities we have. We will be free to enjoy the distinctive Cheerful Despair of those who have taken every fateful fact about life on board.

See also: Jolliness; Pessimism; Resilience; Sentimentality; Splitting and Integration.

¶ Classical

At present, our culture is dominated by a Romantic outlook; its predecessor, and in many ways its more deserving alternative, is a Classical view of life.

Classicism is founded upon an intense, pessimistic awareness of the frailties of human nature and on a suspicion of unexamined instinct. The Classical attitude knows that our emotions can frequently overpower our better insights, that we repeatedly misunderstand ourselves and others, and that we are never far from folly, harm and error.

In response, Classicism seeks via culture to correct the failings of our minds.

Classicism is wary of our instinctive longing for perfection. In love, it counsels a gracious acceptance of the 'madness' inside each partner. It knows that ecstasy cannot last, and that the basis of all good relationships must be tolerance and mutual sympathy. Classicism has a high regard for domestic life; it sees apparently minor practical details as deeply worthy of care and effort; it doesn't think it would be degrading to tidy the laundry cupboard or do the household accounts,

C

because these are modest points at which our own routines intersect with the great themes of life.

Classicism understands that we need rules and, in the education of children, it trusts in the setting of boundaries. It loves, but does not idealise, the young.

In social life, Classicism counsels politeness as a way of keeping our true selves at bay. It understands that 'being yourself' is not something we should ever seek to be around anyone we care for. It also knows that small compliments and reassurances are of huge benefit to us, given our natural frailty and insecurity. It doesn't disdain the writing of thank-you notes.

Classicism believes in evolution rather than revolution. It trusts that many good things have to be accomplished by institutions rather than by heroic lone agents, and accepts the necessary compromises that are involved in working with other people.

In relation to careers, the Classical attitude is at odds with the notion of vocation. It doesn't look to our instincts to solve the complex problems of what we should productively be doing with our lives. Instead it sees the need for careful and extensive self-questioning. But it also assumes from the outset that all work is laborious and frustrating in some ways, rejecting the notion of an 'ideal' job, much as it rejects the ideal in most spheres. It is a fervent believer in the concept of things being 'good enough'.

Unlike Romanticism, Classicism is cautiously welcoming of capitalism. It isn't inherently sceptical of profit; it doesn't see a concern with money as essentially sordid or shameful; money is just a resource that can be used foolishly or wisely. It doesn't think that talking of money is wrong in relation to the issue of who one might marry; it accepts the role of the material in a good life.

Classicism has a particularly ambitious attitude towards art. It sees art as having a mission to seduce us, by means of an alluring, sensuous presentation, to keep wise and useful ideas at the front of our minds. Classical architecture, for instance, is ordered, tranquil and harmonious, because it recognises how vulnerable our inner spirit is to prompts from our environment and accepts how much we stand in need of poise, calm and serenity. It isn't afraid of things being a little boring. A 'quiet life' is no insult for a Classical mind.

Classicism admires compromise around things one doesn't feel like compromising on; it has faith in slow and messy progress rather than in sudden ruptures. It is not shocked by venality, corruption or selfishness (it assumes that these are natural parts of the human character), but likes institutions, rules and laws because of their role in restricting the scope of our impulses.

Although the Classical attitude often conflicts with things that are very popular, it doesn't in any way reject the value of popularity in itself. Indeed, its ambitions are firmly populist. If an idea is very complicated and difficult to grasp, Classicism assumes that it has not yet been brought properly into focus. It is suspicious of the narrows of academia and the cloistering of culture. The ideas we most need, it insists, can be presented lucidly and attractively and must be spread far and with charm to be of any use in taming our chaotic and confused minds. Classicism sees no fundamental reason why wisdom can't be very widespread. Indeed, it takes this to be the definitive, realistic task of civilisation.

The School of Life is built upon a Classical view of existence.

See also: Changing the World; FOMO; Romantic.

¶ Closeness

Even after years with someone, there can be a hurdle of fear about asking for proof that we are wanted – but with a horrible, added complication: we now assume that any such anxiety couldn't possibly exist. This makes it very difficult to recognise our insecure feelings, especially if they have been triggered by a so-called 'small' matter, let alone communicate them to others in ways that would stand a chance of securing us the under-standing and sympathy we crave. Rather than requesting re-assurance endearingly and laying out our longing with charm, we might instead mask our needs beneath some brusque and hurtful behaviours guaranteed to frustrate our aims. Within established relationships, when the fear of rejection is denied, two major symptoms tend to show up.

Firstly, we may become distant – or what psychotherapists call 'avoidant'; we disguise our need for our lover.

Secondly, we may become controlling – or what psycholo-gists term 'anxious'; we disguise our vulnerability behind an officious front.

The solution is to normalise a new and more accurate picture of emotional functioning: to make it clear just how healthy and mature it is to be fragile and in repeated need of reassurance, especially around sex. We suffer because adult life posits too robust a picture of how we operate. It tries to teach us to be implausibly independent and invulnerable. It suggests it might not be right to want a partner to show us they still really like us after they have been away for only a few hours. Or to want them to reassure us that they haven't gone off us, just on the basis that they didn't pay us much attention at a party and didn't want to leave when we did.

Yet it is precisely this sort of reassurance that we constantly need. We are never through with the requirement for comfort. This isn't a curse limited to the weak and the inadequate. In this area, insecurity is a sign of well-being. It means we haven't allowed ourselves to take other people for granted. It means we remain realistic enough to see that things could genuinely turn out badly, and are invested enough to care.

We should create room for regular moments, perhaps as often as every few hours, when we can feel unembarrassed and legitimate about asking for confirmation. 'I really need you; do you still want me?' should be the most normal of enquiries. We should uncouple the admission of need from any associations with the unfortunate and punitively macho term 'neediness'. We must get better at seeing the love and longing that lurk behind some of our and our partner's most frosty, managerial or distant moments.

See also: Anxious Attachment; Avoidant Attachment; Emotional Translation.

¶ Clumsiness

Our clumsiness can feel like one of the most shameful things about us. We spill, fall over, drop, smash … Clumsiness violates our self-image as a competent grown-up. It introduces us to a figure we may have been keen to escape from for a long time: the Inner Idiot.

We are liable to hate our Inner Idiot from afar, with a grim face, and try to deny its reality. But in our clumsy moments, we're reminded that the Idiot is still there, prompting us to drop our phone in the toilet bowl and forget important people's names at a party.

There is a seldom-explored path we might follow to break out of our shame: making friends with the Inner Idiot. Rather than to deny its existence, we might – with a degree of courage and good humour – accept that we simply are, at one level, big idiots who knock things over, spill drinks and make fools of ourselves in small and large ways most days of the year. But this does not, in itself, deny us the right to exist.

Clumsiness constitutes a humiliation if, and only if, we insist that the only way to prove ourselves acceptable is via a constant display of competence. But when we accept the incontrovertible and quasi-universal nature of inner idiocy and clumsiness, the discomfort and self-hatred are lifted. We feel we are alone with our idiocy because of a problem of perspective: we don't see the clumsiness of others as we do our own, because it happens in private and is carefully edited out of public life. Yet it is there in everyone, which is why, on the screen, there is such a widespread appetite for watching people fall off their bikes or walk into lampposts. Thanks to comedy shows, we can experience relief at evidence that desperate clumsiness is not just our own. It may look as if we're mocking; really, we are delighted to have found people as absurd as we are. The best kind of comedy invites us to see our own clumsiness as part of a collective and forgivable foolishness, not a private tragedy.

We see too that our own clumsiness is not what sets us apart from others but what we share (in secret) with everyone. We can accommodate our idiocy more sweetly inside ourselves when we trust that it is an intrinsic feature of being human; that it can be understood and forgiven in ourselves because it must be understood and forgiven in everyone.

If we knew the real lives of others more accurately, we would be much less scared and much less alone.

See also: Confidence; Inner Idiot, The; Inner Voices; Normality; Vulnerability.

¶ Communism

In describing his utopian Communist society, Karl Marx placed enormous emphasis on the idea of everyone having many different jobs. There were to be no specialists here. In a pointed dig at Adam Smith's praise of specialisation, he wrote: 'In communist society... nobody has one exclusive sphere of activity but each can become accomplished in any branch he wishes ... thus it is possible for me to do one thing today and another tomorrow, to hunt in the morning, to fish in the afternoon, rear cattle in the evening, criticise after dinner... without ever becoming a hunter, fisherman, shepherd or critic.' (*The German Ideology*, 1846.)

Marx's solutions to capitalism's problems were evidently awry, but he can be credited for eloquently articulating our longing to do so much more with our lives than a capitalist economy allows. In our hearts, we are far more multiple and promiscuous than it is currently possible to be: beneath the calm outward façade of the accountant might lie someone pining to try landscape gardening. Many a poet might want to work in industry for a few years. Specialisation might be an economic imperative, but it can be a human betrayal.

See also: Specialisation.

¶ Confidence

The way to greater confidence is not to reassure ourselves of our own dignity; it is to come to peace with our inevitable ridiculousness. We are idiots now, we have been idiots in the past, and we will be idiots in the future – and that is okay. There aren't any other available options for human beings.

We grow timid when we become too attached to an idea of our own seriousness and dignity, and are over-exposed to the respectable sides of others. Such are the pains people take to appear normal that we collectively create a phantasm – which hurts everyone – that normality and ongoing dignified competence might be possible.

But once we learn to see ourselves as already, and by nature, foolish, it doesn't matter so much if we do one more thing that might look a touch stupid. The person we try to kiss could indeed think us ridiculous. The individual from whom we asked directions in a foreign city might regard us with contempt. But if these people did so, it wouldn't be news;

they would only be confirming what we had already gracefully accepted in our hearts long ago: that we, like them – and every other person on the earth – are nitwits.

The risk of trying and failing would have its sting substantially reduced. The fear of humiliation would no longer stalk us in the shadows of our minds. We would grow free to try things by accepting that failure was the acceptable norm. And every so often, amid the endless disasters we'd have factored in from the outset, it would work: we'd get a kiss; we'd make a friend; we'd get a raise. The road to greater confidence begins with a ritual of telling oneself solemnly every morning, before heading out for the day, that one is a muttonhead, a cretin, a dumbbell and an imbecile. One or two more acts of folly should, thereafter, not matter much at all.

See also: Clumsiness; Confidence in Confidence; Inner Idiot, The; Normality; Perfectionism; Sane Insanity.

¶ Confidence in Confidence

Although we assume that we must want to be confident, in our hearts, we may harbour suspicions that confidence is in fact an unappealing state of mind. Without fully realising it, we might find the idea of being truly confident strangely offensive, and secretly remain attached to hesitancy and modesty.

Suspicion of confidence has traditionally enjoyed immense cultural endorsement. Christianity – for centuries the greatest influence on the mindset of the West – was highly sceptical about those who think too well of themselves. While the meek basked in divine favour, the arrogant would be the last to enter the kingdom of heaven. The political theory of Karl Marx added to this argument a set of ideas apparently proving that economic success was founded upon the exploitation of others. No wonder it may feel as if – to be moral citizens – we should steer clear of all overly robust assertions of our own interests.

Yet this attitude too can carry dangers. We may lack the confidence not to be cruel and promote greed, but to fight for kindness and wisdom. Our lack of confidence in confidence may be allowing degraded versions of self-assertion to thrive.

Maybe we are just being unfair. Our negative view of confidence can be overly dependent on the quirks of our own histories, or on the sort of people in whom we first encountered confidence, who were not its best or most reliable representatives. Our real problem may not be confidence so much as a lack of other virtues such as manners, charm, wit and generosity. We may be wrongly diagnosing the root of our objections. There may be a danger of growing into braggarts, self-seekers and blowhards. But confidence is in its essence compatible with remaining sensitive, kind, witty and softly spoken. It might be brutishness, not confidence, that we hate.

Furthermore, our attraction to meekness may mask some rather cowardly resentments against self-assertion. We might not so much admire timidity as fear giving confidence a try. It was this species of self-protective deception that particularly fascinated Nietzsche. He thought it a typical error of many Christians, who might pride themselves on their 'forgiveness' while simply trying to excuse their 'inability to take revenge'. We should take care not to dress up our base deficiencies as godly virtues.

Unfortunately, it isn't enough to be kind, interesting, intelligent and wise inside: we need to develop the skill that allows us to make our talents active in the world at large. Confidence is what translates theory into practice. It should never be thought of as the enemy of good things; it is their crucial and legitimate catalyst. We should allow ourselves to develop confidence in confidence.

See also: Confidence.

¶ Consolation

At a collective level, we are deeply committed to the idea of overcoming and resolving problems. We want to banish pain and cure ourselves of the ills of being human.

But there's another less prominent yet highly relevant tradition that doesn't suppose that a share of our most serious problems can ever really be solved. Dying, missing out, failing or losing will not often be amenable to 'solutions' of the sort a scientific and technological age asks us to put our faith in.

The Romantic impulse is to insist that every genuine ill must have an equally potent cure. When facing hardship, we are told that we should redouble our efforts, and never rest until we have altered our destinies. We must rage against the obstacles arrayed against us and overcome them through a bold and stubborn force of will.

Such messages have their place, but they may also, at points, be indistinguishable from cruelty. Kindness lies not only in pushing other people towards solutions; it is also made up of a willingness to console them for the awful but unavoidable presence of tragedy.

The word 'consolation' does not have a good reputation. It sounds like a loser's counsel; something we would be interested in only when other and better options have been exhausted. Yet in relation to some of the largest challenges, consolation is what we need above all else. Sometimes there will simply be no solutions, yet we can be helped nevertheless. We can be comforted by a sense that we are not alone in our suffering; that others care for us; that many have been here before, and that there are reasons – however dark and appalling – why we have ended up in this place. Consolation doesn't seek to tell us that our problems are minor or can be ingeniously worked through. Rather, it dismantles our excessive remaining hopes and reinterprets our particular misery as a feature of a universal and ultimately unavoidable story of woe.

Consolation invites us to look with tenderness on the generic sorrows of humanity of which we have, in time, been allotted our necessary share. Consolation aspires to turn rage and confusion into mourning and melancholy.

See also: Artistic Consolation; Flowers; Jolliness; Melancholy; Sentimentality; Tragedy.

¶ Crushes

A crush plays out in pure and perfect form the dynamics of the Romantic philosophy of love, with its combustible mixture of limited knowledge, outward obstacles to further discovery, and boundless hope.

When we see someone in the street, on the train, or in the library and feel almost at once that they are the answer, we are perhaps not wrong to feel that the stranger has some wonderful qualities, indicated by their eyebrows, quizzical smile or extremely handsome mustard-coloured coat. But our crush ignores a fundamental truth about people that Romanticism blithely ignores: that everyone, even the most apparently accomplished being, is radically imperfect and, were we to spend a long time around them, possibly maddening (even those who have adorable hair or the sweetest way of folding their skirt under them as they sit down on a park bench). We can't yet know what the problems will be, but we can and should be certain that they are there, lurking somewhere behind the façade, waiting for time to unfurl them.

We have to impress this truth upon our Romantic minds – otherwise, in comparison with a crush, every actual relationship we ever have will seem horrendous and doomed. If we truly believe what our imaginations tell us during crushes, we'll have no logical choice other than to break off our partnerships,

C

which are likely to be somewhat disappointing yet deeply real and ultimately 'good enough'.

In order to enjoy a crush we have to understand that that is what it is. If we think that we are encountering a person who will make us happy, who will be an ideal person to live with and grow old with, we are inadvertently destroying the specific satisfaction that a crush brings. The pleasure depends on our recognising that we are imagining an ideal person, not finding a real one.

To crush well is to realise that the lovely person we sketch in our heads is our creation: a creation that says more about us than them. But what it says about us is important. The crush gives us access to our own ideals. We may not really be getting to know another person properly, but we are growing our insight into who we really are.

See also: Cure for Unrequited Love; Incumbent Problem, The; Long-Term Love; Love as Generosity; Romantic Instinct; Splitting and Integration.

¶ Crying with Art

Sometimes works of art move us to tears. We might think this is because what they're showing us is sad, but there's something more peculiar at work. Often, we start crying not when things are horrible, but when they are suddenly and unexpectedly the opposite: when they are unusually sweet, tender, joyful, innocent or kind. Weeping in such circumstances is puzzling, but tells us something important: it's a sign of how hard our lives have become.

Perhaps in a film a father who has been bullying or distant one day turns shyly to his son and admits: 'I always loved you; I never knew how to tell you this; I'm so sorry.' Or in a story we're reading to a child, there might be a page where the penguin tells its friend: 'I will never leave you as long as I live ... '

We cry when art reminds us of what we long for (forgiveness, reconciliation, loyalty) and when it prompts us to remember what we lack. Art evokes all the lost innocence of the world and of our own lives, against which the toughness of things stands out more acutely. The loveliness and goodness on display in art can make the actual ugliness of our existence all the more vivid. We cry at poignant reminders of an elusive paradise, at what we crave for and have been exiled from.

If we were to try creating a robot that could cry at films, with books or at the museum, we would have to do something apparently rather cruel: we would have to ensure that this robot knew about suffering, that it was able to hate itself, to feel confused and frustrated, to ache and hope that it didn't have to ache. It is against this kind of background of pain and sober maturity that beautiful scenes in films or works of art become important rather than merely nice. Our tears tell us something key: that our lives are tougher than they were when we were little, and that our longing for uncomplicated niceness and goodness is correspondingly all the more intense.

See also: Jolliness.

¶ Cultural Mining

Cultural mining describes the process by which the most valuable parts of culture – by which we mean the arts, humanities and philosophy – are recovered from their original contexts and made useful for our own times.

In cultural mining, the refined and practical essence of culture is carefully extracted, cleaned, blasted and remoulded, then used to manufacture those ideas that can best help us to navigate contemporary life.

It has been a historic problem of substantial proportions that hugely valuable cultural insights have often been lodged within highly unappealing material far below 'ground'. It has been dark and cramped in the corridors of culture and hardly anyone other than certain accredited experts has been tempted or allowed to visit. Their labours have had a lot of prestige, but in truth, the material has been like metal in ore: impractical in its raw state.

For culture to be of use to us, it needs to go through a process of refinement, which may involve radical, even drastic, editorial moves. Insights have to be forcefully separated from contexts and then twinned with real-world issues. They must be translated from an arcane language of the deep into a spoken language of the surface. Finally, as in gold mining, only a very small portion of what was originally dug out will ever be usable to make the finished precious item that is sought: in this case, a good idea.

By being treated with immense reverence, and refusing any quick extraction of their essential wisdom, works of culture risk becoming painfully inert in our world. If the genius of Kant's *Critique of Pure Reason* can be grasped only by those who fully comprehend it, then its audience will be reduced to a handful of individuals who have spent their lives mastering the details and cannot preach their wisdom except in terms that are baffling and useless to humanity in general.

The cultural miner knows that preciousness will be the downfall of the best ideas, and is devoted to overcoming its effects.

The School of Life practises Cultural Mining.

See also: Culture Can Replace Scripture; Envy of the Future; Pop Music; Popularisation; Popularity; Seduction.

¶ Culture Can Replace Scripture

When religion began to go into decline in northwestern Europe in the second half of the 19th century, many thoughtful people wondered what would fill the enormous gap it left behind. Where would we derive the consolation and community that religions had once so persuasively offered? How would we learn forgiveness? How could gratitude be instilled? Where would awe come from?

One penetrating answer came from an influential group of intellectuals in France, England and Germany who proposed that there was a highly serviceable, ready-made replacement for Scripture to hand; something that could have all the profundity, utility and emotional reach of the old canon: Culture.

'Culture can replace Scripture' became the new rallying cry of secularising societies. In the novels of Jane Austen and Tolstoy, in the paintings of Chardin and Delacroix, in the music of Schubert and Chopin, it was alleged, there could be just the right material to make up for what humanity was losing through the decline of faith.

It was on this basis that a large number of cultural projects were undertaken with public money: enormous libraries were built, museums were put up that looked like temples ('Museums will be our new cathedrals', was the rallying cry) and humanities departments were started in almost all national universities. Some of what we had once found in a Bible we were now to find in the best novels and epic poems.

The Reading Room of the British Library in London (now part of the British Museum) was built at huge government expense in the 1850s. Not coincidentally, the vast dome was precisely designed to be three feet wider than that of St. Peter's Basilica in Rome – for centuries the largest and most famous church in the world.

In the Netherlands, the Rijksmuseum in Amsterdam, opened in 1885, was designed by the foremost Dutch architect of churches, Pierre Cuypers, and looked (on purpose) almost exactly like a cathedral.

The idea that Culture might replace Scripture is a beautiful and highly valid one. But it is also an idea that, despite the hopes of its earliest proponents, has failed entirely. If one showed up at any museum in the world looking for redemption, solace and friendship (as one might in a religious building), one would become an instant object of suspicion. If one enrolled on a philosophy degree in any university with a view to learning 'how to live and die well' (as the temples once taught one to do), one would be quickly disappointed by the curriculum on offer and probably ejected from the course at an early juncture.

The British Library Reading Room (now part of the British Museum). The architecture of this room deliberately recalls the awe-inspiring and noble spaces of the grandest churches.

The Great Hall, Rijksmuseum, Amsterdam.

Culture truly can deliver wisdom and emotional education, but the guardians of Culture – those who presently control the cultural machine, with its broadcasters, museums and universities – have no interest in honouring this potential. They care instead about the preservation of texts, the display of works, the cataloguing of dates, the analysis of linguistic tropes, and a range of comparable academic pieties. Wisdom, explicit guidance and emotional education are not on the agenda. In the real world, Culture has not replaced Scripture.

Meanwhile, the emotional needs of a secular society remain as intense and as unattended as ever. We have been left to our own devices, without the support of the great public institutions that were originally intended to assist us. The promise of the domed reading rooms and cathedral-like museums remains to be adequately discovered and judiciously exploited.

See also: Akrasia; Art, The Purpose of; Cultural Mining; Philosophy; Popularisation; Popularity; Secularisation; Self-Help Books.

¶ Cure for Unrequited Love

For intense periods of our lives, we suffer the agony of unrequited love. Our sorrow is accompanied by a certainty that
if only the elusive being would return our smiles, come for
dinner or marry us, we would know bliss. Epochal happiness
seems tantalisingly close, wholly real and yet maddeningly
out of reach.

At such moments, we are often counselled to try to forget
the beloved. Given their lack of interest, we should try to
think of something or someone else. Yet this kindness is deeply
misguided. The cure for love does not lie in ceasing to think
of the fugitive lover, but in learning to think more intensely
and constructively about who they might really be.

From close up, every human who has ever lived proves
deeply challenging. At close quarters, we are all trying propositions. We are short-tempered, vain, deceitful, crass, sentimental, woolly, over- or under-emotional and chaotic. What
prevents us from holding this in mind in relation to certain
people is simply a lack of knowledge. On the basis of a few
charming outside details, we assume that the target of our
passion may miraculously have escaped the fundamentals of
the human condition.

They haven't. We just haven't got to know them properly.
This is what makes unrequited love so intense, so long-lasting
and so vicious. By preventing us from properly growing close
to them, the beloved also prevents us from tiring of them in
the cathartic and liberating manner that is the gift of requited
love. It isn't their charms that are keeping us magnetised; it is
our lack of knowledge of their flaws.

The cure for unrequited love is, in structure, therefore
very simple. We must get to know them better. The more we
discovered of them, the less they would look like the solution
to all our problems. We would discover the endless small ways
in which they were irksome; we'd get to know how stubborn,
how critical, how cold and how hurt by things that strike us

as meaningless they could be. If we got to know them better, we would realise how much they had in common with everyone else.

Passion can never withstand too much exposure to the full reality of another person. The unbounded admiration on which it is founded is destroyed by the knowledge that a properly shared life inevitably brings.

The cruelty of unrequited love isn't really that we haven't been loved back; it's that our hopes have been aroused by someone who can never disappoint us, someone who we will have to keep believing in because we lack the knowledge that would set us free.

In the absence of a direct cure, we must undertake an imaginative one. Without quite knowing the details, we must accept that they would eventually prove decisively irritating. Everyone does. We have to believe this, not because we know it exactly of them, but because they are human, and we know this dark but deeply cheering fact about everyone who has ever lived.

See also: Crushes; Incumbent Problem, The.

D

¶ Day of Judgement

Across time, various religions have come up with an idea that, today, can sound extremely odd: the Day of Judgement.

The suggestion has been that, after we die, the merit of our entire lives, with every relevant factor included, will be judged by an all-knowing, all-understanding and ultimately decisive judge: God, perhaps with the help of some angels, against a background of celestial music. Thereafter, the good people will be sent to heaven, the bad ones to hell.

It is a fanciful speculation, but it enforces some eminently sensible and highly important principles of how to live wisely and kindly among others. It operates as a reminder of the dangers of judging each other too readily and confidently, of quickly deciding who is valuable and who can be ignored, of too narrowly settling the question of who is guilty and who innocent.

The theory of the Day of Judgement proposes that the merits and demerits of other people are fundamentally mysterious: important factors about their situation will never be known to us, and we are likely to get things wrong if we rush to assess others' value on the basis of outward markers. It commands us to pause our judgemental proclivities and snobbery and to adopt instead a permanent attitude of modest and kindly neutrality. The Day of Judgement is useful not so much as a prediction about an event that will unfold on the other side of the grave; it matters as a warning to us not to foreclose on people whose true natures and situations we cannot possibly understand as we truly or fairly should.

The Day of Judgement is a strategic counter to the excesses of a meritocratic worldview. Faith in a meritocracy insinuates that we can, without excessive difficulty, judge one another now, almost at a glance, on the basis of what we have achieved, usually in our professional or personal lives. The divorcees and the sacked are the failures in this story; the sick as well.

In fact, where people end up is a desperately and soberingly random matter. Career, romantic and health success reflect only certain parts of who a person is. We might be very witty but not cut out for the top, or be truly extraordinary parents but not very focused on money, or highly imaginative but rather shy, or wise but gravely ill. We might have had a brilliant idea but lack the necessary powers of execution or been cursed by bad timing.

If we judge others too quickly on the outward signs, we may miss the best things about them; they in turn may make the same painful mistake with us. Unfortunately, we don't now have grand and powerful institutions continually reminding us – via magnificent works of art – of the need not to judge too soon, but we can look back at the Day of Judgement as a reminder of a cautious manner of assessing human achievement that, however eccentrically framed it might be, we continue to owe to ourselves and others.

See also: Luck; Meritocracy; Secularisation; Snobbery; Tragedy.

¶ Domesticity

Without our quite noticing it, and to our immense misfortune, the value of domestic life has come to occupy a degraded position in our collective vision of importance.

The pleasures and challenges of managing a household can be made to seem almost comically trivial in comparison to making a great fortune in business, succeeding in sport or entertainment, or occupying a prominent place in the media.

Yet the small, bounded, repetitive issues of the domestic realm play a great part in the essential task of living and dying well. 'If we wish to be happy, we must learn to cultivate our garden' was Voltaire's legendary and deliberately unheroic advice on the matter.

A consequence of our disregard for domesticity is that we often become enraged by what we consider 'small' irritants. Couples fall out spectacularly over whether it is necessary to use a chopping board when cutting bread, how clean the bathroom needs to be or whether it matters if a drawer is left slightly open. What fuels the conflict is a sense that these are trivial matters, unworthy of careful discussion, on which there may be varied and dignified schools of thought.

The fiendish irony is that we behave with exactly this respect around other details that matter much less in our lives. Art historians will hold an international conference on the pose of a hand in a painting by Picasso; huge corporations will devote immense efforts to finding just the right words to announce the merits of a chocolate bar to the world.

We don't always despise details; we are guided by the larger cultural picture of whether a detail deserves attention. Tragically, our culture currently assigns precious little importance to a great many details in the 'garden' of domesticity.

See also: Flowers; FOMO; Getting an Early Night; Glamour; Good Enough; Long-Term Love; Quiet Life, The; Small Pleasures.

¶ Duty Trap, The

We start off in life being very interested in pleasure and fun. In our earliest years, we do little but hunt out situations that will amuse us, pursuing our hedonistic goals with the help of puddles, crayons, balls, teddies, computers and bits and pieces we find in the kitchen drawers. As soon as anything gets frustrating or boring, we simply give up and seek new sources of enjoyment – and no one appears to mind very much.

Then, at around the age of five or six, we are introduced to a terrifying new reality: the Rule of Duty. This states that there are some things we must do, not because we like them or see the point of them, but because other people (intimidating, authoritative people who may be almost three times our size) expect us to do them – so, the big people sternly explain, we'll be able to earn money, buy a house and go on holiday about thirty years from now. It sounds pretty important – sort of.

Even when we're back home and start crying and telling our parents that we don't want to do the essay for tomorrow, they may take the side of Duty and speak to us with anger and impatience – beneath which there is a lot of fear – about how people who can't complete a simple homework assignment on volcanoes (and want to build a treehouse instead) will never survive in the adult world.

Questions of what we actually enjoy doing, what gives us pleasure, still occasionally matter in later childhood, but only a bit. They become matters increasingly set aside from the day-to-day world of study, reserved for holidays and weekends. A basic distinction takes hold: pleasure is for hobbies, pain is for work.

By the time we finish university, this dichotomy is so entrenched that we usually can't conceive of asking ourselves too vigorously what we might really want to do with our lives: what it might be fun to do with the years that remain. It's not the way we've learnt to think. The Rule of Duty has been the governing ideology for 80% of our time on earth – and it's become our second nature. We are convinced that a good job is meant to be substantially dull, irksome and annoying. Why else would someone pay us to do it?

The dutiful way of thinking has such high prestige because it sounds like a road to safety in a competitive and alarmingly expensive world. But the Rule of Duty is actually no guarantee of true security. Once we've finished our education, it emerges as a sheer liability masquerading as a virtue. Duty grows positively dangerous. The reasons are two-fold.

Firstly, it is because success in the modern economy will generally only go to those who can bring extraordinary dedication and imagination to their labours – which is only possible when one is, to a large extent, having fun (a state quite compatible with being exhausted and grumpy most of the time). Only when we are intrinsically motivated are we capable of generating the very high levels of energy and brainpower necessary to stand out from the competition. Work produced merely out of duty is limp and lacking next to that done out of love.

Secondly, when our work is informed by our own sense of pleasure, we become more insightful about the pleasures of others – that is, of the clients and customers a business relies upon. We can best please our audiences when we have mobilised our own feelings of enjoyment.

In other words, pleasure is not the opposite of work; it is a key ingredient of successful work.

Yet we have to recognise that asking ourselves what we might really want to do – without any immediate or primary consideration for money or reputation – goes against our educationally embedded assumptions about what might keep us safe, and is therefore rather scary. It takes immense insight and maturity to stick with the truth: that we will best serve others – and can make our own greatest contribution to society – when we bring the most imaginative and most authentically personal sides of our nature into our work. Duty can guarantee us a basic income. Only sincere, pleasure-led work can generate sizeable success.

D

When people are suffering under the Rule of Duty, it can be helpful to take a morbid turn and ask them to imagine what they might think of their lives from the vantage point of their deathbeds. The thought of death may usefully detach us from prevailing fears of what others think. The prospect of the end reminds us of an imperative higher still than a duty to society: a duty to ourselves, to our talents, to our interests and our passions. The deathbed point of view can spur us to perceive the hidden recklessness and danger within the dutiful path.

See also: Being 'Good'; Meaningful Work; Vocation Myth.

¶ Emotional Capitalism

Emotional Capitalism refers to an economic system that is geared – far more than at present – towards the fulfilment of our higher needs; among these, the needs for emotional health, self-understanding, friendship, consolation and community.

Despite all the factories, highways and logistics chains, the world economy is arguably as yet far too small and desperately undeveloped, for it is still not focused on addressing many of the issues that undermine our well-being. Over the last two centuries, in the wealthy nations, capitalism has evolved to meet many basic material needs, for sanitation, shelter, food supply and healthcare. The largest and most successful corporations have been those that have satisfied appetites that we would categorise as belonging at the bottom of Abraham Maslow's famous pyramid of needs: oil and gas, mining, construction, retail, agriculture, pharmaceuticals, electronics, telecommunications, insurance and banking.

A glance at the pyramid reveals a fascinating possibility: that the future growth of business may lie in meeting the higher needs further up the pyramid, in the areas of love and belonging, esteem and self-actualisation. Capitalists and companies are seemingly – semi-consciously – aware of this issue. The evidence lies in advertising. Advertising almost always tries to sell us goods by tugging obliquely at our longings for emotional fulfilment, authenticity, good relationships and a sense of true achievement.

However, as yet, the corporations who pay for the advertisements are not devoted to meeting the needs that their marketing people have so skilfully evoked. Advertising is always hinting at the future shape of the economy; it already trades on all the right fantasies. It's just that there are, as yet, few of the truly right products and services to satisfy the appetites that have been aroused.

An organised response to our higher needs is not novel. Religions used to address them. Catholicism, if seen as a business, would be the second largest corporation in the world. Art galleries and museums have shared some of the character of religions and similarly have tried to address our higher needs, although their clients have tended to be governments and nations rather than individual customers.

What we call 'a business idea' is at heart an as-yet-unexplored need. To trace the future shape of capitalism, we only have to think of all the needs we have that are poorly understood and neglected by the commercial world. We need help in forming cohesive, interesting communities. We need help in bringing up children. We need help in calming down at key moments (the cost of our high anxiety and rage is appalling in aggregate). We require assistance in discovering our real talents in the workplace and understanding where we can best deploy them. We have unfulfilled aesthetic desires. Elegant town centres, charming high streets and sweet villages are in desperately short supply and are therefore absurdly expensive – just as, prior to Henry Ford, cars existed but were very rare and only for the very rich.

These higher needs are not trivial or minor wants – little things we could easily survive without. In many ways they are central to our lives. We have simply accepted, without really thinking about it, that there is nothing we can do to address them. Yet, to be able to structure businesses around these needs would be the commercial equivalent of the discovery of steam power or the invention of the electric light bulb. We don't know what the businesses of the future will look like, just as no one in 1975 could describe the current corporate essence of Facebook or Google. But we know the direction in which we need to head: we need the drive and inventiveness of capitalism to tackle the higher, deeper problems of life. This will offer an exit from the failings and misery that attend capitalism today. In a nutshell, the problem is that we waste resources on unimportant things. Ultimately, we are wasteful because we lack self-knowledge; we use consumption to divert or quieten anxieties or in a vain search for status and belonging. If we could address our deeper needs more directly, our materialism would be refined and restrained, our work more meaningful and our profits more honourable.

See Also: Good Business; Good Demand; Good Materialism; Higher Needs; Misemployment; Overeating; Secularisation.

¶ Emotional Education

We accept a major role for education at the centre of our societies. We invest hugely in ensuring that knowledge painfully built up in one generation can be reliably transferred to another.

However, our Romantic culture places a curious limit around the idea of what can fairly be taught and transferred. We know that we can teach people how to fly a plane, perform brain surgery or analyse the tax returns of medium-sized businesses – and a host of institutions exist to carry out instruction in these fields.

However, it would sound distinctly odd, even eerie, to imagine that we might learn, for example, how to love someone, how to become wise, how to grow less agitated, or how to die well. Our Romantic culture assumes that in these fields, what we call the area of Emotional Intelligence, we are simply more or less born knowing how to live, and that there is precious little that one human could ever systematically teach another.

Emotional Education is the term given to the contrary belief that we can and must train ourselves in our emotional conduct. We should, its adherents propose, be schooled to respond in more equitable and intelligent ways to our impulses, desires and fears. Emotional Education proposes that emotions are not fixed, unchangeable or even reliable tendencies. We can learn how to be more forgiving; how to extend the range of our sympathies; how to grow more confident, accepting, patient and self-aware.

It is because we have – until now – not taken Emotional Education seriously enough that our species has grown ever more technically adept while retaining the level of wisdom of our earliest days, with catastrophic results. We are evolved monkeys with nuclear weapons. It appears that the fate of civilisation now depends on our capacity to master the mechanisms of Emotional Education before it is too late.

Emotional Education extends far beyond formal education as we have conceived of it to date. Although it should ideally include specialised courses in every year of school or college, Emotional Education is more than something that should take place in classrooms at the hands of teachers and come to a halt around the age of twenty-one.

The central vehicle for the transfer of Emotional Intelligence is culture, from its highest to its most popular level. Culture is the field that can ritualise and consistently promote the absorption of wisdom. The 'lessons' of culture might be embedded in a tragedy or a TV series, a pop song or a novel, a work of architecture or a news bulletin. We can envisage the entire apparatus of culture as a subtle mechanism designed to point us towards greater wisdom.

We will never progress as a species, and will indeed grow into ever-greater technologically armed menaces to ourselves, until we have accepted the challenges and opportunities of Emotional Education.

See also: Emotional Intelligence; Emotional Scepticism; Faulty Walnut, The; Secularisation; Self-Help Books; Transference; Wisdom.

¶ Emotional Intelligence

Emotional Intelligence is the quality that enables us to confront with patience, insight and imagination the many problems that we face in our affective relationship with ourselves and with others.

The term may sound odd. We are used to referring to intelligence as a general quality, without unpicking a particular variety that a person might possess; therefore, we do not tend to highlight the value of a distinctive sort of intelligence that currently does not enjoy the prestige it should.

Every sort of intelligence signals an ability to navigate well around a particular set of challenges: mathematical, linguistic, technical, commercial. When we say that someone is clever but has messed up their personal life, or that they have acquired a fortune but are restless and sad, or that they are powerful but intolerant and unimaginative, we are pointing to a deficit in what deserves to be called Emotional Intelligence.

In social life, we can feel the presence of Emotional Intelligence in a sensitivity to the moods of others and in a readiness to grasp the surprising things that may be going on for them beneath the surface. Emotional Intelligence recognises a role for interpretation and knows that a fiery outburst might be a disguised plea for help; that a political rant may be provoked by hunger; or that concealed within a forceful jolliness may be a sorrow that has been sentimentally disavowed.

In relation to ourselves, Emotional Intelligence shows up in a scepticism around our emotions, especially those of love, desire, anger, envy, anxiety and professional ambition. The Emotionally Intelligent refuse to trust their first impulses or the wisdom of their feelings. They know that hatred may mask love, that anger may be a cover for sadness, and that we are prone to huge and costly inaccuracies in whom we desire and what we seek.

Emotional Intelligence is also what distinguishes those who are crushed by failure from those who can greet the troubles of existence with a melancholy and at points darkly humorous resilience. The Emotionally Intelligent appreciate the role of well-handled pessimism within the overall economy of a good life.

Emotional Intelligence is not an inborn talent. It is the result of education – specifically in how to interpret ourselves, where our emotions arise from, how our childhoods influence us and how we might best navigate our fears and wishes. In the Utopia, it would be routine to be taught Emotional Intelligence from the youngest age, before we have the opportunity to make too many mistakes.

Our Technical Intelligence has led us to tame nature and conquer the planet. A wiser, saner future for the race will depend on our capacity to master and then seductively teach the rudiments of Emotional Intelligence – while there is still time.

See also: Emotional Education; Emotional Scepticism; Inner Voices; Philosophical Meditation; Success at School vs. Success in Life; Wisdom.

¶ Emotional Scepticism

Emotional Scepticism refers to an attitude of good-natured suspicion towards the majority of our first impulses and feelings. The Emotional Sceptic rarely fully trusts what they immediately desire, what they fear and what their so-called 'gut' tells them. They understand their minds to be Faulty Walnuts, highly liable to be throwing off inaccurate or misleading emotions. They like to pause and create a 'fireguard' between their feelings and their actions.

Emotional Sceptics will take their time coming to decisions. They sleep on things. They don't simply act on impulse. They are disinclined to get married after two exceptionally glorious weeks.

Our current culture looks askance at Emotional Scepticism. It sounds very boring, sexless and unimpressive. We are still guided by the Romantic notion that emotions are the voices of our true selves, requiring to be honoured as faithfully and as quickly as possible.

This background ideology explains why there is still so much folly at large – and why Emotional Scepticism is such a priority.

See also: Censorship; Emotional Education; Emotional Intelligence; Faulty Walnut, The; Philosophical Meditation; Politeness; Romantic Instinct; Transference.

¶ Emotional Translation

One of the most deceptive tricks our minds play upon us is to lead us to believe that we know what other people mean just because we can hear their words.

But often what someone is trying to say is very different from what actually comes out of their mouth. We therefore have to undertake a special kind of translation, moving from listening to interpreting.

The need for translation is especially prominent around relationships. Our Romantic culture stresses sincerity and openness, which can make the idea of translation feel like an insult to another person's directness of heart. Yet it may frequently be much kinder and more loving to dig beneath the surface meaning of words in search of a partner's real but more bashful, complex or vulnerable underlying emotional intention.

'I hate you' might not mean this at all; it might be a plea to be noticed and cared for. 'I'm fine' is unlikely to indicate that one is fine; it is almost always a sign that the prospect of revealing one's real complaint and anger has brought on intolerable feelings of weakness and exposure.

In an ideal future, we might wear in our ears little devices of genius that could simultaneously translate people's words into what they actually meant. We would hear (via our discreet, brushed steel appliances) not what they overtly said, but what they were really attempting to communicate.

In the meantime, we must take up the challenge of picking up on hints rather than looking out only for direct statements; we must learn to wisely interpret rather than just to listen to one another.

See also: Closeness; Love as Generosity.

¶ Envy

Envy has been so taboo for so long – at least two thousand years – that some of us are tempted to claim that we 'never feel envy'. Such a pronouncement is psychologically impossible. Envy is a fundamental fact for all of us. The trick isn't simply to suffer from it, but to learn from it.

Envy matters because it can provide us with a host of insights into our potential, our passions and our interests. Every time we envy someone, we are encountering a clue as to who we want to be deep down – and in part probably could be. We don't envy everyone. We envy those who we feel have what we deserve, what we are interested in, and what we could perhaps attain one day. Every person we envy contains suggestions as to our future possible selves.

The real problem isn't that we feel envy, but that we envy in such unexamined and fruitless ways. Firstly, we feel deeply embarrassed by our envy, and so tend to hide the emotion from our conscious selves. Secondly, we don't have faith that there is anything to be learnt from envy, and so we hope the mood will pass, like a vicious fever.

Thirdly, we start to envy certain individuals in their entirety, when, if we took a moment to analyse their lives calmly, we would realise that it was only a small part of what they had done that really resonated with, and could guide, our own next steps. It might not be the whole of the restaurant entrepreneur's life we wanted, but really just their skill at building up institutions. We might not truly want to be a potter, yet we might need a little more of the playfulness on display in the work of one example we read about in a supplement.

The more we drill into our envy, the less attached we need to be to the actual lives of the people who triggered it.

The qualities we admire don't just belong to the very specific, very attractive locations in which we discovered them. These qualities can be pursued in lesser, weaker (but still real) doses in countless other places, opening up the possibility of creating many smaller, more manageable and more realistic versions of the lives we admire.

See also: Job Fixation.

¶ Envy of the Future

When we look widely across the past, we can feel strange waves of compassion for the immense numbers of people who were condemned – by the sheer misfortune of when they happened to be born – to appalling varieties of suffering that are now easily avoided. Their lives might have been destroyed by an illness that can now be prevented by a shot of the cheapest vaccine; they laboured under terrifying convictions we now regard as baseless illusions. A child might die of hunger on the very land now occupied by a bountiful supermarket. Their misery was so profound, and yet, from where we stand, so preventable. They would have envied us, if they could have realised what we have.

But there is another thought that might emerge: that at some point a future society might look back on our mode of life with similar feelings of pity. They might hear stories of our fractious relationships, which so often end in divorce, and feel immense tenderness for our unnecessary suffering – avoided by them via careful counselling, digital head implants and inter-cranial education from birth about how to manage the complexities of life with another person. They may look sorrowfully on our working lives, in which we so rarely feel that what we are doing is truly important; or at the difficulty we have in finding and keeping true friendships; or at the regularity with which families prove disappointing.

When we think of envying the future, we are primed to do so in terms of technology. Future humans might be able to vacation on Mars or look youthful when they are two hundred and three. But the real poignancy may turn out to be psychological.

Our successors may master the art of being somewhat less dissatisfied, angry, confused, bored and vengeful.

The pity we imagine they might experience for us is really an echo of the pity we should legitimately feel for ourselves. We are registering ways in which our lives are genuinely sorrowful in comparison with what they might be.

But the good news is that the future does not really depend on technological breakthroughs; it could, curiously and tantalisingly, start to be available now, if only we could learn to act upon the vast reserves of wisdom our species has already so carefully and so painfully accumulated.

See also: Akrasia; Cultural Mining; Utopia.

¶ Equality and Envy

We are repeatedly told that we are equal. This sounds like a great idea, but it carries an unexpected psychological burden. The reality is that we are equal before the law, equal in rights, but we are definitely not equal in our circumstances. The modern age combines an ideology of equality with radical material inequality.

This has led to a proliferation of envy. Envy is a curious emotion in that we don't feel it in relation to everyone who has more than us. We envy those who have more than us and to whom we feel equal. Nowadays we would be unlikely to feel envious of a member of the British monarchy. Their world is too remote from our own, their accents too odd, their characters alien. Despite them having much more than us, despite their palaces, carriages and art works, we can consider their lives without the slightest distress. However, when we hear of someone our age, with a slightly larger apartment than ours, a somewhat more dynamic career and an ability to send their children to a slightly better school, our envy may grow boundless and quasi-obsessive.

It is the feeling of equality, and not just differences in wealth and achievement, that drives envy. The closer two people feel, the more equal they are in each other's eyes, and the more any divergence of success will have the power to dispirit and enrage them. And the problem with the modern world is that it constantly informs us that we are all equal deep down, while simultaneously holding up for our torture examples of people who have secured uncommon degrees of fame and wealth for themselves.

In the old world, it would not have occurred to any ordinary person to envy an aristocrat or monarch. These exalted characters lived in separate realms and went to great lengths to show the rest of the world how different they were, and how inconceivable it was that one could ever get to be like them. Their clothes, habits and ways of life made it clear that one should never assume they were normal in any way.

Louis XIV of France liked to wander about in ermine cloaks and gold brocade coats. He carried a golden stick. He sometimes donned a suit of armour. It was extremely haughty and unfair, of course, but it did have one great advantage. You could not possibly believe that you, in all your profane ordinariness, would ever reach the summit. You couldn't possibly envy the mighty, because envy only begins with the theoretical possibility that one might be rightfully owed what the envied person already has.

By contrast, modernity was founded on an apparently generous sense that everyone is owed the same things. Not in terms of current possessions and status, but in terms of potential. Yet it then performed a particularly challenging move: it made sure that we don't all end up having the same things. It combined the sense of possibility with the reality of inequality, and so opened up a new terrain of suffering.

See also: Expectations; Meritocracy; Suicide.

¶ Eudaimonia

Eudaimonia is an Ancient Greek word, particularly empha-sised by the philosophers Plato and Aristotle, that deserves wider currency. It corrects the shortfalls in one of the most central, governing but insufficient terms in our contemporary idiom: *happiness.*

When we nowadays try to articulate the purpose of our lives, it is to the word 'happiness' that we commonly have recourse. We tell ourselves and others that the ultimate rationale for our jobs, our relationships and the conduct of our day-to-day lives is the pursuit of happiness. It sounds like an innocent enough idea, but excessive reliance on the term means that we are frequently unfairly tempted to exit or at least heavily question a great many testing but worthwhile situations.

The Ancient Greeks resolutely did not believe that the purpose of life was to be happy; they proposed that it was to achieve eudaimonia, a word that has been best translated as 'fulfilment'.

What distinguishes happiness from fulfilment is pain. It is eminently possible to be fulfilled and, at the same time, under pressure, suffering physically or mentally, overburdened and frequently tetchy. This is a psychological nuance that the word 'happiness' makes it hard to capture, for it is tricky to speak of being happy yet unhappy or happy yet suffering. However, such a combination is readily accommodated within the dig-nified and noble-sounding letters of eudaimonia.

The word encourages us to trust that many of life's most worthwhile projects will at points be quite at odds with con-tentment and yet are worth pursuing nevertheless. Properly exploring our professional talents, managing a household, keeping a relationship going, creating a new business ven-ture or engaging in politics – none of these goals is likely to leave us cheerful and grinning on a quotidian basis. They will involve us in all manner of challenges that will exhaust and enervate us, provoke and wound us. Yet we will, perhaps, at the end of our lives, still feel that the tasks were worth undertaking. Through them, we will have accessed something grander and more interesting than happiness: we will have made a difference.

With the word eudaimonia in mind, we can stop imagining that we should aim for a pain-free existence, and then berate ourselves unfairly for being in a bad mood. We will know that we are trying to do something far more important than smile: we are striving to do justice to our full human potential and to work in some small but key way towards the improvement of our species.

See also: Artistic Consolation; Meaning of Life, The; Pessimism; Resilience; Self-Help Books.

¶ Existential Angst

We are frequently thrown into states of extreme anxiety by our need to make a choice between options, in situations where we lack the necessary information and cannot be certain of the future. We are in a state of what is known as Existential Angst.

At such moments, it pays to remember that the real choice is almost never between error and happiness but between varieties of suffering. This is the wisdom of the early 19th-century Danish Existential philosopher Søren Kierkegaard, summed up in a playful, but bleakly realistic and exasperated, outburst in his masterpiece, *Either/Or:*

> Marry, and you will regret it; don't marry, you will also regret it; marry or don't marry, you will regret it either way. Laugh at the world's foolishness, you will regret it; weep over it, you will regret that too; laugh at the world's foolishness or weep over it, you will regret both. Believe a woman, you will regret it; believe her not, you will also

regret it … Hang yourself, you will regret it; do not hang yourself, and you will regret that too; hang yourself or don't hang yourself, you'll regret it either way; whether you hang yourself or do not hang yourself, you will regret both. This, gentlemen, is the essence of all philosophy.

We deserve pity – as does everyone else. We will make disastrous decisions, we will form mistaken relationships, we will embark on misguided careers, we will invest our savings foolishly and spend years on friendships with unreliable and disappointing knaves. But we can be consoled by a bitter truth: we have no better options, for the conditions of existence are intrinsically rather than accidentally frustrating.

There is, curiously, a persistent relief to be found in the knowledge of the inevitability of suffering. In the end, it is not darkness that dooms us, but the wrong sort of hope.

See also: Pessimism; Resilience.

¶ Expectations

High expectations are the secret cause of many of our agonies. We are not always humiliated by failing at things; we are only humiliated if we first invested our pride and sense of worth in a given achievement and then did not reach it. Our expectations determine what we will interpret as a triumph and what must count as a failure. 'With no attempt there can be no failure; with no failure no humiliation. So our self-esteem in this world depends entirely on what we back ourselves to be and do,' wrote the psychologist William James; 'it is determined by the ratio of our actualities to our supposed potentialities. Thus:

$$\text{Self-esteem} = \frac{\text{Success}}{\text{Expectations}},$$

The problem with the modern world is that it does not stop lending us extremely high expectations. We are constantly invited to dream. Today, you may be short of cash, low on prestige and bruised by rejection. But, it is insinuated, these are transient troubles. Hard work, a positive attitude and bright ideas have every chance of breaking the deadlocks in due course. It is just a question of willpower. Modernity never ceases to emphasise that success could, somehow, be ours one day. In this way, it never ceases to torture us.

See also: Equality and Envy; Good Enough; Lottery of Life; Luck; Perfectionism; Work/Life Balance.

F

¶ Fame

Fame seems to offer very significant benefits. The fantasies go like this: when you are famous, wherever you go, your good reputation will precede you. People will think well of you, because your merits have been impressively explained in advance. You will get warm smiles from admiring strangers. You won't need to make your own case laboriously on each occasion. When you are famous, you will be safe from rejection. You won't have to win over every new person. Fame will mean that other people will be flattered and delighted even if you are only slightly interested in them. They will be amazed to see you in the flesh. They will ask to take a photo with you. They will sometimes laugh nervously with excitement. Furthermore, no one will be able to afford to upset you. When you're not pleased with something, it will become a big problem for others. If you say your hotel room isn't up to scratch, the management will panic. Your complaints will be taken very seriously. Your happiness will become the focus of everyone's efforts. You will make or break other people's reputations. You'll be the boss.

The desire for fame has its roots in the experience of neglect and injury. No one would want to be famous who hadn't also, somewhere in the past, been made to feel insignificant. We sense the need for a great deal of admiring attention when we have been painfully exposed to earlier deprivation. Perhaps one's parents were hard to impress. They never noticed one much, they were so busy on other things, focusing on other famous people, unable to have or express kind feelings, or just working too hard. There were no bedtime stories and one's school reports weren't the subject of praise and admiration. That's why one dreams that one day the world will pay attention. When we're famous, our parents will have to admire us too (this throws up an insight into one of the great signs of good parenting: that your child has no desire to be famous).

But even if our parents were warm and full of praise, there might still be a problem. It might be that it was the buffeting and indifference of the wider world (starting with the schoolyard) that was intolerable after the early years of adulation at home. One might have emerged from familial warmth and been mortally hurt that strangers were not as kind and understanding as one had come to expect. The crushing experience of humiliation might even have been vicarious: one's mother being rudely dismissed by a waiter; one's father standing awkwardly alone.

What is common to all dreams of fame is that being known to strangers emerges as a solution to a hurt. It presents itself as the answer to a deep need to be appreciated and treated decently by other people.

Yet fame cannot accomplish what is asked of it. It does have advantages, which are evident. But it also introduces a new set of very serious disadvantages, which the modern world refuses to view as structural rather than incidental. Every new famous person who disintegrates, breaks down in public or loses their mind is judged in isolation, rather than being interpreted as a victim of an inevitable pattern within the pathology of fame.

One wants to be famous out of a desire for kindness. But the world isn't generally kind to the famous for very long. The reason is basic: the success of any one person involves humiliation for lots of others. The celebrity of a few people will always contrast painfully with the obscurity of many. Being famous upsets people. For a time, the resentment can be kept under control, but it is never somnolent for long. When we imagine fame, we forget that it is inextricably connected to being too visible in the eyes of some, to bugging them unduly, to coming to be seen as the plausible cause of their humiliation: a symbol of how the world has treated them unfairly.

Soon enough, the world will start to go through the rubbish bags of the famous; it will comment negatively on their appearance; it will pore over their setbacks; it will judge their relationships; it will mock their new movies.

Fame makes people more, not less, vulnerable, because it throws them open to unlimited judgement. Everyone is wounded by a cruel assessment of their character or merit. But the famous have an added challenge in store. The assessments will come from legions of people who would never dare to say to their faces what they can express from the safety of the newspaper office or screen. We know from our own lives that a nasty remark can take a day or two to process.

Psychologically, the famous are the last people on earth to be well equipped to deal with what they're going through. After all, they only became famous because they were wounded, because they had thin skin; because they were in some respects a bit ill. Now, far from compensating them adequately for their disease, fame aggravates it exponentially. Strangers will voice their negative opinions in detail, unable or unwilling to imagine that famous people bleed far more quickly than anyone else. They might even think that the famous aren't listening (although one wouldn't become famous if one didn't suffer from a compulsion to listen too much).

Every worst fear about oneself (that one is stupid, ugly, not worthy of existence) will daily be confirmed by strangers. One will be exposed to the fact that people one has never met, about whom one would have only goodwill, actively loathe one. One will learn that detestation of one's personality is a badge of honour in some quarters. Sometimes the attacks will be horribly insightful. At other times, they'll make no sense to anyone who really knows one. But the criticisms will lodge in people's minds nevertheless – and no lawyer, court case or magician can ever delete them.

Needless to say, as a hurt celebrity, one won't be eligible for sympathy. The very concept of a hurt celebrity is a joke, about as moving for the average person as the sadness of a tyrant.

To sum up: fame really just means you get noticed a great deal, not that you are understood, appreciated or loved.

At an individual level, the only mature strategy is to give up on fame. The aim that lay behind the desire for fame remains important. One still wants to be appreciated and understood, but the wise person accepts that celebrity does not actually provide these things. Appreciation and understanding are only available through individuals one knows and cares about, not via groups of a thousand or a million strangers. There is no shortcut to friendship, which is what the famous person is in effect seeking.

For those who are already famous, the only way to stay sane is to stop listening to what the wider world is saying. This applies to the good things as much as to the bad. It is best not to know. The wise person knows that their products need attention. But they make a clear distinction between the purely practical needs of marketing and advocacy and the intimate desire to be liked and treated with justice and kindness by people they don't know.

At a collective, political level we should pay great attention to the fact that, today, so many people (particularly young ones) want to be famous – and even see fame as a necessary condition for a successful life. Rather than dismiss this wish, we should grasp its underlying worrying meaning: they want to be famous because they are not being respected, because citizens have forgotten how to accord one another the degree of civility, appreciation and decency that everyone craves and deserves. The desire for fame is a sign that an ordinary life has ceased to be good enough.

The solution is not to encourage ever more people to become famous, but to put massive efforts into encouraging a greater level of politeness and consideration for everyone, in families and communities, in workplaces, in politics, in the media, and at all income levels, especially modest ones. A healthy society will give up on the understandable but erroneous belief that fame might guarantee the kindness of strangers.

See also: Love as Generosity.

¶ Fashion

Once, we were all dressed by someone else. Parents picked out a T-shirt; the school dictated what colour our trousers should be. But at some point, we were granted the opportunity to discover who we might be in the world of clothes. We had to decide for ourselves about collars and necklines, fit, colours, patterns, textures and what goes (or doesn't go) with what. We learnt to speak about ourselves in the language of garments.

Despite the potential silliness and exaggeration of sections of the fashion industry, assembling a wardrobe is a serious and meaningful exercise.

Based on our looks, background, job or certain tendencies in our behaviour, others are liable to come to quick and not very rounded decisions about who we are. Only too often, their judgement doesn't get us right. They might assume that, because of where we come from, we must be quite snobbish or resentful; based on our work we might get typecast as dour or superficial; the fact that we're sporty might lead people to see us as not terribly cerebral; an attachment to a particular political outlook might be associated with being unnervingly earnest or cruel.

Clothes provide us with an opportunity to correct some of these assumptions. When we get dressed, we are, in effect, operating as a tour guide, offering to show people around ourselves. We're highlighting interesting or attractive things about who we are – and we're clearing up misconceptions in the process.

We're acting like artists painting a self-portrait: deliberately guiding the viewer's perception of who we might be. Clothes are a way of making a crucial introduction to the self. This explains the curious phenomenon whereby, if we're staying with good friends, we can spend a lot less time thinking about our clothes, compared with the anxiety about what to wear that can grip us at other times. We might sit around in a dressing gown. They already know who we are; they're not relying on our clothes for clues.

By choosing particular sorts of clothes, we are shoring up our more fragile or tentative characteristics. We're communicating to others who we are and strategically reminding ourselves. Our wardrobes contain some of our most carefully written lines of autobiography.

See also: Architecture; Good Materialism.

¶ Faulty Walnut, The

The phrase 'the Faulty Walnut' makes affectionate reference to the instrument that sits on top of our spinal cords, an organ that is hugely powerful, inventive, nimble, capable of astonishing calculation and conjecture and – at the same time – dangerously and pervasively flawed. Paradoxically, the way to greater lucidity is not to place ever deeper faith in our walnuts; it is to keep their misleading, exaggerated and deceptive nature constantly at the forefront of our thoughts. Wisdom begins with a recognition of certain of our fundamental inclinations to folly and blindness.

The walnut is marked by a range of stubborn defects that are dangerously hard to extirpate, let alone recognise in good time. It is prone to desiring and fearing without properly assessing reality. It doesn't understand its own motives or pleasures. It quickly locks onto answers and is vain and squeamish around the arduous business of self-examination. When pressed for clarification, it typically grows blank or aggressive. It is slyly expedient, preferring short-term sentimental peace to hard long-term truths. It is constantly derailed – in ways it haughtily refuses to recognise – by hormones, low sugar levels and tiredness. It doesn't readily accept its physical nature, and often petulantly resists an imperative to get an early night. It is deeply marked by its early childhood experiences in ways it can't fathom without many hours of adult introspection (which it is generally disinclined to invest in). It repeatedly transfers emotions from the past onto the present, where they don't quite belong, and thereby over- or under-reacts to situations in the here and now. It is structurally unable to count its own blessings and is overwhelmingly focused on the future. It is wired for perpetual anxiety and nagging dissatisfaction.

All the more pity then, that we inhabit an essentially Romantic culture that proclaims its awe of the power of our brains and is reverent towards their first verdicts and schemes – what we call our 'instincts'. We hear that it is good to 'trust our feelings', that reason is 'cold' and that there are dangers we might end up 'thinking too much' (rather than, as is always the case, merely thinking very badly, which is a different thing).

When we follow our walnuts' instinctive promptings, our lives threaten rapidly to come undone: we don't pay sufficient attention to our biases and blindspots; we become entangled in relationships that repeat harmful childhood patterns; we pursue careers unsuited to our true yet unknown natures; we waste a lot of time on things that don't properly satisfy us …

Compensation for the flaws of our minds is the task of Culture. Culture, which includes the arts, education and politics, can be in a position to counter-balance the eccentricities and foolishness of our walnuts. Culture can alert us to our flaws, make us cautious around our instincts and instil better habits of thinking and feeling. It should endlessly, and with great charm, tug us away from our first, emotional responses and guide us seductively towards wiser, more patient, attitudes.

The art of living lies in knowing how, at an individual and societal level, to manage the melodramas and whims of the Faulty Walnuts through which we wonkily apprehend reality.

See also: Addiction; Censorship; Emotional Education; Emotional Scepticism; Genius; Monasteries; Philosophical Meditation; Resilience; Romantic Instinct; Transference; Wisdom.

¶ Flowers

It is extremely rare properly to delight in flowers when one is under twenty-two. There are so many larger, grander things to be concerned about than these small, delicately sculpted, fragile and evanescent manifestations of nature: for example, romantic love, career fulfilment and political change.

However, it is rare to be left entirely indifferent by flowers after the age of fifty. By then, almost all one's earlier aspirations will have taken a hit, perhaps a very large one. One will have encountered some of the intractable problems of intimate relationships. One will have suffered the gap between one's professional hopes and the available realities. One will have had a chance to observe how slowly and fitfully the world ever alters in a positive direction. One will have been fully inducted to the extent of human wickedness and folly – and to one's own eccentricity, selfishness and madness.

By then, flowers will have started to seem somewhat different; no longer a petty distraction from a mighty destiny, no longer an insult to ambition, but a genuine pleasure amid a litany of troubles, an invitation to bracket anxieties and keep self-criticism at bay, a small resting place for hope in a sea of disappointment. Flowers are a proper consolation for which one is ready, a few weeks of the year, to be appropriately grateful.

We learn to garden, and grow satisfied with our bounded lot, when we have learnt the perils of the wide pitiless fields.

See also: Bounded Work; Consolation; Domesticity; Quiet Life, The.

¶ FOMO (Fear Of Missing Out)

FOMO is the strong sense that life is elsewhere, leading to restlessness with one's condition and a sense of ingratitude towards everything one is and has.

The catalysts of FOMO are everywhere. We are continually bombarded with suggestions about what we might do (go jet skiing, study in Colorado, visit the Maldives or see the Pyramids) or where the really extraordinary parties, cities and jobs might be. The modern world makes sure we know at all times just how much we're missing. It is a culture in which intense and painful doses of FOMO are almost inevitable.

There are, fundamentally, two ways in which the brute facts of missing out can be viewed: one can take a Romantic or a Classical approach.

To the Romantic temperament, missing out causes agony. Somewhere else, noble, interesting and attractive people are living exactly the life that should be ours. We would be so happy if only we could be over there, at that party, with those people, or working in that agency off Washington Square, or holidaying in that shack in Jutland. Sometimes it may make us want to burst into tears.

The Romantic believes in the idea of a defined centre where the most exciting things are happening. At one time it was New York, for a few years it was Berlin, then London. Now, it's probably San Francisco; in five years it may be Auckland or Rio.

For the Romantic, humanity is divided into a large group of the mediocre and a tribe of the elect: artists, entrepreneurs, the edgy part of the fashion world and the people doing creative things with tech. As a Romantic, it can be exhausting inside our soul. Our mother sometimes drives us to fury: her life is utterly dull. How can she accept it? Why isn't she itching to move to the Bay area? She's always suggesting we take a job in Birmingham or inviting us on walking holidays in the Lake District. Sometimes we are quite rude to her. We avoid certain people like the plague: the shy friend from school who struggles with their weight; the flatmate who is a telecoms engineer and wants to go into local politics. Being around individuals who are so unglamorous and lacking in ambition can feel fatal.

For their part, Classically minded people acknowledge that there are, of course, some genuinely marvellous things going on in the world, but they doubt that the obvious signs of glamour are a good guide to finding them. The best novel in the world, they like to think, is probably not currently winning prizes or storming up the bestseller lists. It may be being written at this moment by an arthritic woman living in the otherwise unremarkable Latvian town of Liep ja.

Classical people are intensely aware that good qualities coexist with some extremely ordinary ones. Everything is jumbled up. Lamentable taste in jumpers is compatible with extraordinary insight. Academic qualifications can give no indication of true intelligence. Famous people can be dull. Obscure ones can be remarkable. At a perfect launch party, drinking sandalwood cocktails at the coolest bar in the world, one could feel sad and anxious. One might have the deepest conversations of one's life with an aunt – even though she likes watching snooker on television and has stopped dyeing her hair.

The Classical temperament also fears missing out, but has a rather different list of things they are afraid of not enjoying: getting to truly know one's parents; learning to cope well with being alone; appreciating the consoling power of trees and clouds; discovering what their favourite pieces of music really mean to them; chatting to a seven-year-old child ... As these wise souls know, one can indeed miss out on some extremely important things if one is always rushing to find excitement elsewhere.

See also: Classical; Domesticity; Romantic.

G

¶ Genius

We hear a lot about genius. We are taught to admire the minds of those infinite, baffling but astonishing geniuses such as Einstein, Tolstoy or Picasso.

But what genius might actually be is left a little vague. It is a code word for 'brilliant but perhaps too other-worldly ever really to fathom'. We are invited to stand in awe at the achievements of geniuses but also to feel that their thought processes might be quasi-magical and that it is simply mysterious how they were able to come up with the ideas they had.

But there is a radically different view, suggested by a hugely prescient quote from the 19th-century American genius Ralph Waldo Emerson: 'In the minds of geniuses, we find – once more – our own neglected thoughts.'

What this tells us is that the genius doesn't have different kinds of thoughts from the rest of us. They simply take them more seriously. We ourselves will often have had our own sketchy, hesitant version of their ideas, which is why their works can make such a distinctive impression on us. What they present feels surprising and impressive, yet also obvious and right once it has been pointed out. They are giving clear and powerful articulation to notions that are already familiar because we've been circling them ourselves, possibly for years, without being able to close in on them properly.

In this sense, genius can be defined as paying closer attention to our real thoughts and feelings and being brave and tenacious enough to hold onto them even when they find no immediate echo in the world beyond. The reason why we disavow so much of what passes through our minds is in essence anxiety. We kill off our most promising thoughts for fear of seeming strange to ourselves and others. This explains why small children are, in their own way, so much more interesting than the average adult: they have not yet become experts in what not to say or think.

But when we censor and close down, when we take fright and try not to think, is exactly the moment when the so-called genius starts to take note of what is happening within them.

We operate with a false picture of genius when we identify it too strongly with what is exotic and utterly beyond us. It is something far more provocative than this. Genius is what we all can be when we pay careful attention to what is passing through our consciousness. We all have very similar and very able minds; where geniuses differ is in their more robust inclinations to study them properly and hold on more bravely to their contents.

See also: Faulty Walnut, The; Romantic.

¶ Getting an Early Night

To a surprising, and almost humiliating, extent some of the gravest problems we face during a day can be traced back to a brutally simple fact: that we have not had enough sleep the night before.

The idea sounds profoundly offensive. There are surely greater issues than tiredness. We are likely to be up against genuine hurdles: the economic situation, politics, problems at work, tensions in our relationship, the family …

These are true difficulties. But what we often fail to appreciate is the extent to which our ability to confront them with courage and resilience is dependent on a range of distinctly 'small' or 'low' factors: what our blood sugar level is like, when we last had a proper hug from someone, how much water we've drunk – and how many hours we've rested.

We tend to resist such analyses of our troubles. It can feel like an insult to our rational, adult dignity to think that our sense of gloom might stem from exhaustion. We would sooner identify ourselves as up against an existential crisis than see ourselves as sleep-deprived.

We should be careful of under- but also of over-intellectualising. To be happy, we require large serious things (money, freedom, love), but we need a lot of semi-insultingly little things too (a good diet, hugs, rest).

Anyone who has ever looked after babies knows this well. When life becomes too much for them, it is almost always because they are tired, thirsty or hungry. With this in mind, it should be no insult to insist that we never allow ourselves to adopt a truly tragic stance until we have first investigated whether we need to have some orange juice or lie down for a while.

Probably as a hangover from childhood, 'staying up late' feels a little glamorous and even exciting; late at night is when (in theory) the most fascinating things happen. But in a wiser culture than our own, some of the most revered people in the land would, on a regular basis, be shown taking to bed early. There would be competitions highlighting sensible bedtimes. We would be reminded of the pleasures of already being in bed when the last of the evening light still lingers in the sky. Our problems would not thereby disappear, but our strength to confront them would at points critically increase.

See also: Domesticity; Glamour; Small Pleasures; Warmth.

¶ Glamour

Glamour is the reflexive sheen afforded to people and things by the approval of the most prestigious sectors of society. What we like is not as spontaneous as we think. Our sense that something is exciting or admirable is intimately tied to the degree of glamour it is able to lay claim to. To put it another way: it is immensely hard for us to dare to like things that lack glamour.

G

Sir David Wilkie, *George IV*, 1829.
The novelist Sir Walter Scott was so able to imbue the kilt with glamour that King George IV had his portrait painted while wearing one.

Glamour, flowing from the endorsement of high-status figures, is conveyed along the most prestigious avenues of fashion, literature and the arts. A TV series can bestow glamour on a whole region of the planet, such as the uplands of Patagonia, or on a whole era of history, such as the 1960s. The most popular novelist of the early 19th century, Sir Walter Scott, briefly made kilts glamorous; his sovereign, King George IV, even wore one in an official portrait.

Things are constantly gaining or losing glamour. Many not especially helpful things can end up glamorous: founding a tech company, being very slim, being very angry, always saying what you think immediately, family skiing holidays … And many very helpful things are not glamorous at all: small gestures of kindness, learning poems by heart, coping with having the wrong sort of nose, being polite, doing the laundry … The lack of glamour makes it harder for us to get enthusiastic about these moves or devote ourselves to them with a modicum of grace.

Rather than reject glamour, the priority is to redirect it more accurately. In the Utopia, the following things would be glamorous: forgiveness, depressive realism, the acceptance of imperfection, humility and gratitude. In other words, glamour would support, rather than undermine, the pursuit of a good life.

Fortunately, it has always been possible to raise the esteem of hitherto disregarded things. With effort, the light of glamour can be redirected. Even an examined life might, one day, be artfully rendered glamorous.

See also: Advertising; Domesticity; Getting an Early Night; Normality; Seduction; Wisdom.

¶ Good Brands

The word 'brand' brings with it disturbing associations: heartless commercialism, crushing uniformity, blandness, a dumbed-down experience. A brand can be seen as a cynical way of cashing in on what might once have been a good idea by stripping away whatever was originally quirky, authentic and brave and churning out a standardised product. It is the corporate antithesis of art. When anyone sells out, it's a brand that buys their soul.

G

There are plenty of bad brands around, so it's understandable that blame gets attached to the underlying notion of the brand itself. It becomes tempting to suppose that, ideally, we would live in an unbranded world. In fact, the idea of a brand is a really significant one. A good economy needs good brands.

Essentially, a brand is a constellation of qualities; it is a personality in the material realm. It presents a vision of life in a hugely condensed manner. But a brand doesn't only symbolise a set of ideas. It makes these ideas reproducible and universal. Brands allow particular qualities to multiply across the world. We tend to be alive to the negative possibilities, but the true culprit is never the pure idea of repetition. What we tend really to be objecting to is what is being repeated.

In the 16th century, the Italian architect Andrea Palladio worked out some basic designs for villas, churches and public buildings in the Classical style. He built the first version in the little town of Vicenza. But his ideas spread; they were branded and universalised. Over the centuries, they were taken up in France, the UK, Poland, Russia and especially in the US. Thomas Jefferson in particular bought into the Palladian brand: his own house, Monticello, and the University of Virginia are key examples of franchise architecture, just as much as is the design for a McDonald's restaurant. The key issue isn't free creativity versus the cold hand of the brand. Rather, it's between the good, noble brand (like Palladio) and the less impressive versions that tend to be much more familiar.

Brands invite the recognition that great things are rarely done by individuals acting in heroic isolation. At some point, every good idea, every important insight should go through the process of becoming a brand, so as to widen its power. The world is in great need of better brands.

See also: Good Business; Good Demand; Good Materialism.

¶ Good Business

Good Business is a form of economic activity that has two ends in view: to make money and to satisfy the higher needs of humankind.

This dual target makes good business doubly hard to succeed at. Most organisations have only one goal in view: they either try to make money without regard for higher needs, or they target higher needs without regard for money.

Both of these choices come at a great cost: either profit becomes dissociated from true human value, or the beneficial influence of an organisation is undermined by its financial weakness.

The future of business lies in learning to make profits from our higher rather than our lower needs.

In the Utopia, business would have the same moral cachet that today attaches to charity, and for the same reason: its core efforts would be directed to improving the lives of others.

See also: Advertising; Artistic Philanthropy; Emotional Capitalism; Good Brands; Good Demand; Good Materialism; Higher Needs; Misemployment; Utopia.

¶ Good Demand

The sort of work that is available to us and the societies we live in are largely the result of an issue that is humblingly small and close to home: what we decide to spend our money on. The combined purchasing choices of millions of people profoundly shape the nature of employment, the structure of remuneration and the distribution of prestige. The term 'consumer' capitalism acknowledges that we live in economies substantially defined by what we want to buy.

Governments are used to carefully tracking demand, and panic at signs of its decline. When there is a sharp shortfall, they will move to stimulate consumption so as to ward off dire consequences for employment, tax revenue and investment confidence.

But we should note the extent to which government focus is always on the quantity of demand, not its quality. It is considered more or less irrelevant what people are spending money on, so long as they are spending. They might be buying doughnuts or taking French conversation classes, seeing a psychotherapist or purchasing sports cars. In terms of GDP, unemployment and the stock market, the nature of demand doesn't matter, so long as the total spend is high.

Yet, in other ways, it matters immensely what we spend our money on, because what we buy determines what kinds of lives we will end up leading and, most importantly, what sorts of jobs there will be; whether they will be degrading or noble, useful to others or noxious. This is where a major statement of value can come in: there is better and worse demand. Demand for guns is less 'good' than demand for education. Demand for healthy food is better than demand for its junk alternative. Good Demand might be defined as an aggregate of consumer choices in line with a generous, fruitful understanding of higher human needs.

Good Demand has been elusive because it is so hard for us to identify our higher needs. We are prone to grasping at whatever is blinking most intensely and attractively at us. We are creatures of the herd and will buy what others are buying. We are also surrounded by a hugely active industry that artfully encourages us to want things for its benefit rather than our own. Advertising is founded on our inability to hold on to an accurate picture of our true needs.

Our failures mean that, individually, we may not get the happiness we seek. Collectively, we will end up with a profoundly dysfunctional economy. Raising the quality of demand doesn't imply a draconian government imposing a high-minded agenda on a reluctant public. In a market-oriented democratic society, change can only ever be voluntary. Altering demand can't be a matter of forcing anyone to do anything. What we need is the more important, more humane, task of encouraging ourselves to live up to our own highest aspirations in our purchasing choices. The result will be nobler kinds of profit, and fewer dissatisfied and meaning-poor working lives.

See also: Advertising; Emotional Capitalism; Good Brands; Good Business; Good Materialism; Higher Needs; Misemployment; Utopia.

¶ Good Enough

The mid-20th-century English psychoanalyst, Donald Winnicott, who specialised in working with parents and children, was disturbed by how often he encountered in his consulting rooms parents who were deeply disappointed with themselves. They felt they were failing as parents and hated themselves intensely as a result. They were ashamed of their occasional rows, their bursts of short temper, their times of boredom around their own children and their many mistakes. They were haunted by a range of anxious questions: are we too strict, too lenient, too protective, not protective enough? What struck Winnicott, however, was that these people were almost always not at all bad parents. They were loving, often very kind, and very interested in their children; they tried hard to meet their needs and to understand their problems as best they could. As parents they were – as he came to put it in a hugely memorable and important phrase – 'good enough'.

Winnicott identified a crucial issue. We often torment ourselves because we have in our minds a very demanding, and in fact impossible, vision of what we're supposed to be like across a range of areas of our lives. This vision doesn't emerge from a careful study of what actual people are like; it's a fantasy, a punitive perfectionism, drawn from the cultural ether.

When it comes to parenting, we imagine a fantasy of parents who are always calm, always perfectly wise, always there when their child needs them. There are no parents like this. But a Romantic conception of the perfect parent can fill our minds and make us deeply anxious and fretful, because our own family life inevitably looks so messy and muddled by comparison. Astonishingly and unreasonably inflated expectations leave us only able to perceive where we have fallen short.

With the phrase 'good enough', Winnicott was initiating a hugely important project. He wanted to move us away from idealisation. Ideals may sound nice, but they bring a terrible problem in their wake: they can make us despair of the merely quite good things we already do and have. 'Good enough' is a cure for the sickness of idealisation.

Winnicott introduced the idea of 'good enough' around parenting. But it applies widely across our lives, because we idealise around a great many different things. For example, we might refer to the 'good enough' job. It may not meet our fantasy demands: creative yet secure; fascinating yet unstressful; morally uplifting yet highly paid. But by the standards of what real jobs are like, it might be OK and worth taking pride in. Or we could speak of the 'good enough' marriage. It might not be the perfect union of two souls, sex may be intermittent,

G

there may be regular frustrations and misunderstandings and a fair number of flare-ups. But by the standards of actual long-term relationships, that might be genuine success.

By dialling down our expectations, the idea of 'good enough' resensitises us to the lesser, but very real, virtues we already possess, but that our unreal hopes have made us overlook.

A 'good enough' life is not a bad life. It's the best existence that actual humans are ever likely to lead.

See also: Domesticity; Expectations; Jolliness; Normality; Perfectionism; Procrastination; Splitting and Integration; Wisdom; Work/Life Balance.

¶ Good Materialism

When people seek to pinpoint the root cause of corruption in our age, they generally need only to point to our attachment to material things. We are sick because we are so profoundly materialistic.

It can seem as if we're faced with a stark choice: to be materialistic – obsessed with money and possessions, shallow and selfish – or to reject materialism, be good and focus on more important matters of the spirit.

Most of us are stuck somewhere between these two choices. We are still enmeshed in the desire to possess while hating ourselves for being so.

Crucially, it's not actually materialism – the pure fact of buying things and getting excited by possessions – that is really the problem. We're failing to make a clear distinction between good and bad versions of materialism.

Let's try to understand good materialism through a slightly unusual route: religion. Because we see religions as focused exclusively on spiritual things, it can be surprising to note how much use they have made of material things. They have spent a lot time making and thinking about shrines, temples, monasteries, art works, scrolls to hang in houses, clothes and ceremonies.

However, they have wanted material things to serve the highest and noblest purpose: the development of our souls. It is just that they have recognised that we are incarnate, sensory, bodily beings, and that the way to get through to our souls must be through our bodies rather than merely through the intellect.

For centuries, the importance of material things was at the core of Christianity, which proposed that Jesus was both the highest spiritual being, and a flesh and blood person. He was the spirit incarnate; holiness embodied.

In the Catholic Mass, great significance is accorded to bread and wine, which are believed to be transubstantiations of Christ: that is, material objects that simultaneously have a spiritual identity, just as Jesus himself combined the spiritual and the bodily while on earth.

This can sound like an arcane point entirely removed from the local shopping mall, but exactly the same concept applies outside of religions. Many good material possessions can be said to involve a kind of 'transubstantiation', whereby they are both practical and physical and also embody or allude to a positive personality or spirit.

One can imagine a handsome wooden chair that 'transubstantiates' a set of important values: straightforwardness, strength, honesty and elegance. By getting closer to the chair, we could become a little more like it.

Material objects can be said to play a positive psychological (or spiritual) role in our lives when higher, more positive, ideals are 'materialised' in them. Therefore, buying them and using them daily gives us a chance to get closer to our better selves. When they are contained in physical things, valuable psychological qualities that are otherwise often intermittent in our thoughts and conduct can become more stable and resilient.

This is not to say that all consumerism is unproblematic; it depends on what a given material object stands for. An object can transubstantiate the very worst sides of human nature – greed, callousness, the desire to triumph – as much as it can the best. So we must be careful not to decry or celebrate all material consumption: we have to ensure that the objects we invest in, and tire ourselves and the planet by making, are those that lend encouragement to the best sides of our natures.

See also: Emotional Capitalism; Fashion; Good Brands; Good Business; Good Demand; Home.

¶ Good Nationalism

To many people, Nationalism sounds suspicious – dangerously close to jingoism and racism. But the desire to feel proud of one's community is a natural and noble impulse. We just need sophisticated ways of directing our urge for pride.

Collective pride is important because there is never enough to be proud of in a single life. Nationalism takes the pressure off us to be individually accomplished and admirable. It lightens the oppressive responsibility we might otherwise feel to ensure that our own lives could always be stellar and heroic; that's why patriotism often appeals to those who have the narrowest opportunities.

In an ideal, utopian society, nationalism would be a powerful sentiment, but it would be focused on things that don't normally figure in national anthems or patriotic speeches. In the future, the nationalist might love their country for things such as: the general elegance and harmony of cities; the way you don't have to be rich to live in a gracious neighbourhood; the low divorce rate brought about not by sullen resignation but because of the collective investment in the stages leading up to marriage, and the sophisticated support provided by the state when things get tricky in families. People would be proud that, in their nation, they consume a lot of elderflower cordial rather than alcohol; have a public honours system that rewards displays of wisdom; that the richest person in the country is a psychoanalyst; and that they have a global reputation for being tactful.

What we worry about isn't, in truth, pride in a country but vanity about things that aren't truly admirable. The solution to nationalism isn't to abolish it (which isn't viable anyway), but to create in a society things in which wise people could rightly take pride.

See also: Saints; State Broadcasting.

¶ Higher Needs

What humans require to survive and thrive can roughly, but usefully, be arranged in a hierarchy that runs from lower to higher needs, stretching from the need for food and shelter to the need for self-understanding, meaning and connection.

Business is the foremost instrument through which we attempt to satisfy needs nowadays. But if we analyse economic activity, we find that the overwhelming proportion of it lies clustered around the satisfaction of our lower needs. The large enterprises focus nearly exclusively on catering to such needs as those for transport and nutrition, housing and heating, communication and logistics. Meanwhile, our higher needs lie in a pre-industrial disorganised condition, in the hands of gurus and inspirational teachers, outside the mechanisms and useful disciplines of the market.

This presents a vast economic opportunity for the future. We will in time learn to commercialise all our more complicated needs, which will result in a more honourable and meaningful form of capitalism. Although it might look as if the economy as it stands is well developed, when measured against our real requirements for happiness, we have barely scratched the surface, and an enormous expansion of capitalism is at hand. We plainly need not only food and shelter but, among many other things, to live in beautiful cities; to have good advice and psychological support; to manage our emotions; to sustain strong families across generations; to cultivate our minds; to be wise, kind and self-possessed; and to be the recipients of news and entertainment that are reliably well targeted to our requirements for inner growth and dignity.

Each of these presents immense targets for the businesses of the future to aim for. The fact that these needs don't look the same as those that led to the construction of highways or pipelines doesn't make them illegitimate or unviable. It is no corruption of higher needs to ask that commerce begins to address them; rather, it is an attempt to make capitalism as meaningful as it can be.

See also: Advertising; Emotional Capitalism; Good Business; Good Demand; Misemployment.

¶ History

We tend to be very gloomy about our own era: the state of society seems lamentable; the international situation is dire; the political process unnerving; commercial society rapacious; the media hysterical and vulgar; and education in crisis. We feel we are living in terrible times.

But 'terrible' in comparison to what? The media constantly invites us to view how things are today against a very narrow slice of time. Things feels worse than they were yesterday or last week or two years ago, before the most recent atrocity, economic downturn or security crisis.

By contrast, what we call History offers us a much bigger, fairer and more consoling comparison across large slices of time. It frames what is happening now against the perspective of how things normally tend to go over decades and centuries.

It teaches us some usefully dark lessons. We learn that societies are almost never very admirable; there are always crises; economies pretty much always fluctuate; manners and morals are always shifting and in some ways getting worse; almost no human communities have ever been remarkably just or equal; progressive moments never quite achieve what was hoped of them and are almost always followed by periods of reaction.

Nevertheless, History also reminds us that things have seemed close to outright collapse many times before but that eventually humanity has more or less pulled through. The Roman Empire was governed for many years by a string of horrendous emperors such as Nero and Caligula. But this didn't signal the end of everything, although sometimes it must have seemed as if it would. The chaotic years were followed a bit later by a succession of able and honourable governments (including that of the philosopher Marcus Aurelius) and long periods of civilised prosperity. The troubles of our own times

Ludolf Bakhuizen, *Warships in a Heavy Storm,* c. 1695.
Like this ship weathering rough seas, civilisations almost always survive turbulent times.

are – much more than we tend to suppose – at once very normal and much less fatal than we are inclined to imagine.

A society at any time can be likened to a ship in a storm. A striking thing about the painting by the 17th-century Dutch artist Ludolf Bakhuizen is that it doesn't show a ship sinking. It is a painting of a ship managing to hold its own in frightening circumstances that it has been adroitly designed to withstand. It's a distinction we easily miss. To a sailor on a first voyage, it would, understandably, have felt as if violent death were imminent. But as the older crew would know, the ships of the Dutch navy had survived many far worse storms already.

In effect, the news is always trying to place us in the position of the first-time voyager. It is always stoking our natural panic for its own commercial ends (there is no money to be made from reassuring audiences that things will be OK). By contrast, History is like the person who has been on the seas for many years and can therefore compare any one storm with many others.

History is an artificial, laboriously constructed, beautiful corrective to the natural short-term perspectives of our timid and alarmed minds.

See also: News.

¶ History is Now

It can be hard to imagine how we might change the status quo. Much that is around us conspires to give off a sense of fixity. We are surrounded by institutions and habits that have lasted for centuries. We trust that the human beings who came before us have fully mapped the range of the possible. If something hasn't happened, it's either because it can't happen or it shouldn't.

When we study History, however, the picture changes sharply. Once time is speeded up and we climb up a mountain of minutes to survey the centuries, change appears constant. New continents are discovered; alternative ways of governing nations are pioneered; ideas of how to dress and whom to worship are transformed. Once people wore strange cloaks and tilled the land with clumsy instruments. A long time ago, they chopped a king's head off. Way back, people got around in fragile ships, ate the eyeballs of sheep, used chamber pots and didn't know how to fix teeth.

We come away from all this knowing, in theory at least, that things do change. However, in practice, and almost without noticing, we tend to distance ourselves and our own societies from a day-to-day belief that we belong to the same ongoing turbulent narrative and are, at present, its central actors. History, we feel, is what used to happen; it can't really be what is happening around us in the here and now. In our vicinity at least, things have settled down.

To attenuate this insensitivity to the omnipresence of change and, by extension, the passivity it breeds, we might turn to some striking lines in T.S. Eliot's cycle of poems, *Four Quartets* (1943):

So, while the light fails
On a winter's afternoon, in a secluded chapel
History is now and England.

Winter afternoons, around 4pm, have a habit of feeling particularly resolved and established, especially in quiet English country chapels, many of which date back to the Middle Ages. Hence the surprise of Eliot's third line, his resonant: 'History is now and England'. In other words, everything that we associate with history – the impetuous daring of great people, the dramatic alterations in values, the revolutionary questioning of long-held beliefs, the upturning of the old order – is still going on, even at this very moment, in outwardly peaceful, apparently unchanging places like the countryside near Shamley Green in Surrey, where Eliot wrote the poem. We don't see it only because we are standing far too close to it. The world is being made and remade at every instant. Any one of us has a theoretical chance of being an agent in history, on a big or small scale. It is open to our own times to build a new city as beautiful as Venice, to change ideas as radically as the Renaissance, to start an intellectual movement as resounding as Buddhism.

The present has all the contingency of the past – and is every bit as malleable. It should not intimidate us. How we love, travel, approach the arts, govern, educate ourselves, run businesses, age and die are all up for further development. Current views may appear firm, but only because we exaggerate their fixity. The majority of what exists is arbitrary, neither inevitable nor right, simply the result of muddle and happenstance. We should be confident, even at sunset on winter afternoons, of our power to join the stream of history – and, however modestly, change its course.

¶ Home

One of the most meaningful activities we are ever engaged in is the creation of a home. Over a number of years, typically with a lot of thought and considerable dedication, we assemble furniture, crockery, pictures, rugs, cushions, vases, sideboards, taps, door handles and so on into a distinctive constellation that we anoint with the word 'home'. As we create our rooms, we engage passionately with culture in a way we seldom do in the supposedly higher realms of museums or galleries. We reflect profoundly on the atmosphere of a picture; we ponder the relationship between colours on a wall; we notice how consequential the angle of the back of a sofa can be, and ask carefully what books truly deserve our ongoing attention.

Our homes will not necessarily be the most attractive or sumptuous environments we could spend time in. There are always hotels or public spaces that would be a good deal more impressive. But after we have been travelling a long while, after too many nights in hotel rooms or in the spare rooms of friends, we typically feel a powerful ache to return to our own furnishings – an ache that has little to do with material comfort per se. We need to get home to remember who we are.

Creating a home is frequently such a demanding process because it requires us to find our way to objects that can correctly convey our identities. We may have to go to enormous efforts to track down what we deem to be the 'right' objects for particular functions, rejecting hundreds of alternatives that would, in a material sense, have been perfectly serviceable, in the name of those we believe can faithfully communicate the right messages about who we are.

H

We get fussy because objects are, in their own ways, hugely eloquent. Two chairs that perform much the same physical role can articulate entirely different visions of life. An object feels 'right' when it speaks attractively about qualities that we are drawn to, but don't possess strong enough doses of in our day-to-day lives. The desirable object gives us a more secure hold on values that are present yet fragile in ourselves; it endorses and encourages important themes in us. The smallest things in our homes whisper to us; they offer us encouragement, reminders, consoling thoughts, warnings or correctives, as we make breakfast or do the accounts in the evening.

The quest to build a home is connected with a need to stabilise and organise our complex selves. It's not enough to know who we are in our own minds. We need something more tangible, material and sensuous to pin down the diverse and intermittent aspects of our identities. We need to rely on certain kinds of cutlery, bookshelves, laundry cupboards and armchairs to align us with who we are and seek to be. We are not vaunting ourselves; we're trying to gather our identities in one receptacle, preserving ourselves from erosion and dispersal. Home means the place where our soul feels that it has found its proper physical container, where, every day, the objects we live among quietly remind us of our most authentic commitments and loves.

See also: Architecture; Good Materialism.

¶ Impostor Syndrome

In many challenges, both personal and professional, we are held back by the crippling thought that people like us could not possibly triumph given what we know of ourselves: how reliably stupid, anxious, gauche, crude, vulgar and dull we really are. We leave the possibility of success to others, because we don't seem to ourselves to be anything like the sort of people we see lauded around us.

The root cause of Impostor Syndrome is a hugely unhelpful picture of what other people are really like. We feel like impostors not because we are uniquely flawed, but because we fail to imagine how deeply flawed everyone else is beneath a more or less polished surface.

The Impostor Syndrome has its roots in a basic feature of the human condition. We know ourselves from the inside, but others only from the outside. We are aware of all our anxieties, doubts and idiocies from within. Yet all we know of others is what they happen to do and tell us – a far narrower and more edited source of information.

The solution to Impostor Syndrome lies in making a crucial leap of faith: that, despite a lack of reliable evidence, everyone else must be as anxious, uncertain and wayward as we are. The leap means that whenever we encounter a stranger, we are not really encountering a stranger, we are encountering someone who is – despite the surface evidence to the contrary – very much like us. Therefore, nothing fundamental stands between us and the possibility of responsibility, success and fulfilment.

See also: Psychological Asymmetry.

¶ Incumbent Problem, The

The Incumbent Problem refers to the vast, but often over-looked and unfair, advantage that all new people, cities and jobs have over existing – or, as we put it, incumbent – ones. The beautiful person glimpsed briefly in the street as we step off the bus; the city visited for a few days on holiday; the job we read about in a few tantalising paragraphs of a magazine – these have unwise tendencies to seem immediately and definitively superior to our current partner, our long-established home and our committed workplace and can inspire us to sudden and sometimes regrettable divorces, relocations and resignations.

When we spot apparent perfection, we tend to blame our spectacular bad luck for the mediocrity of our lives, without realising that we are mistaking an asymmetry of knowledge for an asymmetry of quality; we are failing to see not that our partner, home and job are especially awful, but that we know them especially well.

Incumbents are the victims of disproportionate knowledge. They are generally no worse than anyone or anything else, but as they are familiar, their every failing has had a chance to be minutely charted.

The corrective to disproportionate knowledge is experience. We need to mine the secret reality of other people and places and so learn that, beneath their charms, they will almost invariably be essentially 'normal' in nature: that is, no worse yet no better than the incumbents we already understand.

The solution to the Incumbent Problem is to extrapolate from what we already know and apply it to what we don't yet know. The most plausible generalisation we can make about unknown things is that they are likely to be closer to what we've already experienced than they are to being completely and bountifully different.

We should beware of the injustices we unthinkingly visit upon all the incumbent features of, and relationships in, our lives.

See also: Crushes; Cure for Unrequited Love.

¶ Infidelity

Infidelity is commonly interpreted as close to the greatest tragedy that could befall any relationship, and as the natural, inevitable prelude to the break-up of a union.

It is viewed in such dark terms because, under the philosophy of Romanticism, which has dominated our understanding of love since the middle of the 18th century, sex is understood to be not principally a physical act but the summation and central symbol of love. Before Romanticism, people had sex and fell in love, but they did not always see these two acts as inextricably linked: one might love someone and not sleep with them, or sleep with them and not love them. It was this dislocation that Romanticism refused to countenance. Sex was simply the crowning moment of love, the superlative way of expressing one's devotion to someone, the ultimate proof of one's sincerity.

What this philosophy unwittingly accomplished was to turn infidelity from a problem into a catastrophe. Never again could sex be viewed as being divorced from intense emotion and a profound desire for commitment. It was no longer possible to say that sex meant 'nothing', in the sense of being a joyful, kind but emotionally empty act devoid of any desire to care for or live with a new person in the long term and in no way indicative of any drop in affection for the established partner.

There are, of course, many cases where infidelity means exactly what Romanticism takes it to mean: contempt for one's relationship. But in many other cases, it may mean something rather different: a passing, surface desire for erotic excitement that coexists with an ongoing, sincere commitment to one's life partner.

Our culture makes this thought close to impossible, so 'getting over' an infidelity – by which is meant, learning to see that the unfaithful act might not mean what Romanticism tells us it means – has become a challenge of heroic proportions and, most of the time, a brute impossibility. However much an unfaithful partner may patiently explain that it meant nothing, the idea seems entirely implausible. How could sex, the summation of love, ever mean anything less than pretty much everything?

There may be one potential way out of the impasse: a frank examination of the recesses of one's own mind and, perhaps, an honest recall of certain moments of past personal experience. What this brave investigation is likely to throw up is evidence that one is strangely capable of something rather surprising: caring deeply for someone and yet entertaining, or masterminding, a sexual scenario involving somebody else. However much the thought seems unbelievable when we hear it from the mouth of a straying partner, in some ways it seems quite possible to think of screwing one person and loving another.

The best way to recover after an infidelity may therefore be to ignore what Romanticism tells us that infidelity has to mean, and to consult a more reliable source of information: what we ourselves took infidelity to mean the last time the idea crossed through our minds or our lives. It is on this basis that we may – with considerable pain, of course – come to be able to forgive and even in a way understand and accept the apologies of a repentant partner. It is on the basis of subjective experience of unfaithful thoughts that we may redemptively enrich, complicate and soften what happens when we end up as their victims.

See also: Secrets in Love; Sex and Love.

¶ Inner Idiot, The

The 'Inner Idiot' is a bracing term used to describe a substantial, hugely influential and strenuously concealed part of everyone. An Idiot is what we deeply fear being; it is what we suspect in our darkest hours that we might be; and it is what we should simply accept, with humour and good grace, that we often truly are. A decent life isn't one in which we foolishly believe we can slay or evade the Inner Idiot; it's one in which we practise the only art available to us: sensible cohabitation.

The Inner Idiot makes itself felt at moments small and large. The Idiot is clumsy: it forgets names, loses important documents, spills food down its front and gets air kisses wrong. It speaks out of turn, thrusts itself forward at inopportune moments, both babbles and blushes. The Idiot is prickly, it gets into a rage because it was momentarily ignored, it sees plots against it where there was only accident, it shouts when a drawer won't open properly and is immediately self-righteous when faced with the most minor criticism. It is, for the Idiot, always someone else's fault. The Inner Idiot is a child on a bad day.

We know our own Inner Idiot from the inside and might suppose it is unique to us. In fact, it represents what might be called the 'lower' self of all of humanity. It is only residual good manners that has made the Inner Idiot of others less obvious to us – and hence made our own seem like a freakish exception.

Much of wisdom consists in accepting that the Inner Idiot will never go away and that we should therefore endeavour to form a good working relationship with it.

Trying to prevent the emergence of the Inner Idiot otherwise inspires a range of unfortunate traits. For example, we may lose confidence and grow unnecessarily meek and cautious in a bid to appear dignified and serious in front of others. We may refuse ever to ask someone for a date or for a pay rise;

we might never go travelling on our own or give a speech in public, as all of these moves require a calculated risk of being hijacked by the Idiot.

By denying our Idiot, we may grow unfeasibly pompous and stiff. Nothing makes us seem absurd faster than insisting on our own seriousness. We are always better off confessing to idiocy in good time, rather than letting it emerge from behind our carefully constructed pretensions.

In relationships, there can be no greater generosity than to tell a partner, early on, what our Inner Idiot is like, to give them a road map to its antics, and to apologise promptly and warmly when it has overwhelmed us. None of us should try to find a partner who lacks an Inner Idiot (it's impossible); we should just find out more about the particular kind of Idiot they have. In a wiser world, an entirely standard and wholly inoffensive question on an early dinner date would be: 'And what is your Inner Idiot like?'

By squaring up to the existence of the Inner Idiot, we may come to feel a useful compassion for ourselves. Of course we made a mess of certain things; of course we made some bad decisions; of course we said the wrong things. What else could we have done, given that we are hosting a powerfully idiotic being in our minds and that our rational cleverness and goodness sit precariously on top of its many deeply unintelligent impulses?

We may spread our compassion to others as well. They were not necessarily evil when they hurt us; they merely possess a domineering Idiot of their own.

The best school for learning about the Inner Idiot is comedy. The essence of comedy is to expose the workings of the Idiot in a way that invites sympathetic laughter rather than harsh criticism. The stand-up artist is a sage who knows how to redescribe their Idiot with accurate benevolence, and teaches us to do the same.

Love is another solution to the problems of the Inner Idiot. In its most mature and desired sense, love means encountering and embracing the Idiot of another, regarding it not with horror or as an affront, but with all the imagination and generosity with which a parent might look upon their beloved red-faced two-year-old in a tantrum.

It's not very nice that we have an Inner Idiot. In fact, it's an immense inconvenience. But we cannot wish the issue away. A wise society would be ambitious about understanding, accommodating and forgiving the Inner Idiot in everyone, and would be devoted to finding ways to soothe it and limit its influence. In the Utopia, there would be classes in schools and headline government policies focused entirely on helping us admit – without too much shame – the presence of our and others' Inner Idiots and then instructing us with patient determination how to work around their flaws as best we can.

It is one of the greatest of all human achievements when we can finally move from seeing someone as an 'Idiot' to being able to consider them as that far less offensive and more morally hybrid creature: a 'Loveable Idiot'.

See also: Clumsiness; Confidence; Normality; Other-as-Child; Universal Love; Vulnerability.

¶ Inner Voices

We all have Inner Voices in our minds. They talk to us as we try to achieve things or deal with our lives. Sometimes they are kind, but often they are punitive, telling us we're stupid or worthless or that we deserve every misfortune that comes our way.

An Inner Voice was always once an outer voice that we have imperceptibly made our own. Perhaps we have absorbed the tone of a harassed or angry parent; the menacing threats of an elder sibling keen to put us down; the contempt of a schoolyard bully, or the words of a teacher who seemed impossible to please. We take in these voices because, at certain key moments in the past, they sounded compelling and irresistible. The dominant figures of our individual histories repeated their messages over and over until they became lodged in our own way of thinking – sometimes to our great cost.

The ideal Inner Voice doesn't pretend that everything we do is wonderful. Rather, it is like the voice of an ideal friend. These figures can recognise when we have done something unwise, but they are merciful, fair, accurate in understanding what's going on and interested in helping us deal with our problems. It's not that we should stop judging ourselves; the hope is that we can learn to be better judges of ourselves.

Instead of promoting a self-flagellating critical internal commentary, a good friend represents a calm, constructive way of addressing failings.

Culture has a role to play here. If our surrounding culture is broadcasting voices that are at once realistic and supportive, complex and morally perceptive, it will be much easier for us to adopt this manner internally as we comment on the trickier parts of our own lives. External generous wisdom can take up residence in the place it is most needed: our private running conversation with ourselves.

See also: Art, The Purpose of; Clumsiness; Emotional Intelligence; Self-Sabotage; Tragedy; Transitional Object.

¶ Insomnia

Insomnia is seldom a disease: it is an inarticulate, maddening but ultimately almost logical plea released by our core self, asking us to confront certain issues we've put off for too long. Insomnia isn't really to do with not being able to sleep; it's about not having given ourselves a chance to think.

It is the revenge of all the many thoughts we didn't take seriously enough in the day.

See also: Philosophical Meditation; Unprocessed Emotion.

J

¶ Job Fixation

A Job Fixation is a determination to secure a particular kind of job that, for one reason or another, turns out not to be a promising or realistic option. It may be that the job is difficult to attain, it may require long years of preparation, or it might be in an industry that has become precarious and therefore denies us good long-term prospects.

We call it a fixation – rather than simply an interest – to signal that the focus on the job is problematic because we have an overwhelming sense that our future lies with this one occupation and this occupation alone, while facing a major obstacle in turning our idea into a reality. The solution to such fixations lies in coming to understand more closely what we are really interested in: the more accurately and precisely we fathom what we really care about, the more we stand to discover that our interests exist in a far broader range of occupations than we have until now been entertaining.

It is our lack of understanding of what we are really after – and therefore our relatively standard and obvious reading of the job market – that has pushed us into a far narrower tunnel of options than is warranted.

The careful investigation of what we love in one field of work shows us – paradoxically but liberatingly – that we could also love working in a slightly different field.

We may find that what we really love isn't this specific job, but a range of qualities we have first located there. This job was the most conspicuous example of a repository of those qualities, which is where the problem started: over-conspicuous jobs tend to attract too much attention, are over-subscribed and offer only very modest salaries.

Yet in reality, the qualities can't only exist in that one job. They are necessarily generic and will be available under other, less obvious guises – once we know how to look.

See also: Envy; Vocation Myth.

¶ Jolliness

Jolliness might sound like an ideal state of mind. However, with its remorseless and insistent upbeat quality, it has little in common with what is really required for a well-lived life.

Normality includes a lot of sorrows. Many genuinely sad things occur in every existence, pretty much every day. In the background of most of our lives, there is likely to be a powerful sadness. It's natural to want to skirt contact with it, but such avoidance comes at a high price. Honesty about the darkness inside ourselves and the strangeness and cruelty of life more generally are crucial components in engaging with our own ambitions and achieving intimacy with others.

In a discussion of parenting styles, the psychoanalyst Donald Winnicott once identified a particularly problematic kind of child carer: the person who wants to 'jolly' babies and small children along, always picking them up with cheer, bouncing them up and down and pulling exaggerated funny faces, perhaps shouting 'peekaboo' repeatedly. The criticism might feel disconcerting: what could be so wrong with wanting to keep a child jolly? Yet Winnicott was worried by what effect this would have on a child – the way it was subtly not giving the child a chance to acknowledge its own sadness, or more broadly, its own feelings.

The jollier doesn't just want the child to be happy; more alarmingly, it can't tolerate the idea that it might be sad, so unexplored and potentially overwhelming are his or her own background feelings of disappointment and grief.

Childhood is necessarily full of sadness (as is adulthood), insisted Winnicott, and we must perpetually be granted the possibility of periods of mourning: for a broken toy, the grey sky on a Sunday afternoon, or the lingering sadness we can see in our parents' eyes.

We need a public culture that remembers how much of life deserves to have solemn and mournful moments and that isn't tempted – normally in the name of selling us things – aggressively to deny the legitimate place of melancholy.

See also: Artistic Consolation; Cheerful Despair; Consolation; Crying with Art; Good Enough; Kintsugi; Melancholy; Normality; Sentimentality; Unprocessed Emotion; Vulnerability.

K

¶ Kintsugi

Kin = golden
tsugi = joinery

The origins of Kintsugi are said to date to the Muromachi period, when the Shogun of Japan, Ashikaga Yoshimitsu (1358–1408), broke his favourite tea bowl. Distraught, he sent it to be repaired in China. On its return, he was horrified by the ugly metal staples that had been used to join the broken pieces, and charged his craftsmen with devising a more appropriate solution. What they came up with was a method that didn't disguise the damage, but made something honestly artful out of it.

Kintsugi belongs to the Zen ideals of *wabi-sabi,* which cherishes what is simple, unpretentious and aged – especially if it has a rustic or weathered quality. A story is told of one of the great proponents of wabi-sabi, Sen no Rikyū (1522–1599). On a journey through southern Japan, he was invited to a dinner by a host who thought he would be impressed by an elaborate and expensive antique tea jar that he had bought from China. But Rikyū didn't even seem to notice this item and instead spent his time chatting and admiring a branch swaying in the breeze outside. In despair at this lack of interest, once Rikyū had left, the devastated host smashed the jar to pieces and retired to his room. But the other guests more wisely gathered the fragments and stuck them together through kintsugi. When Rikyū next came to visit, the philosopher turned to the

Tea bowl, porcelain with gold lacquer repairs, early 17th century.
The aesthetic of Kintsugi lends reverence to the damaged and imperfect –
a principle we could usefully employ in our own lives.

repaired jar and, with a knowing smile, exclaimed: 'Now it is magnificent'.

In an age that worships youth, perfection and the new, the art of kintsugi retains a particular wisdom – as applicable to our own lives as to a broken teacup. The care and love expended on the shattered pots should lend us the confidence to respect what is damaged and scarred, vulnerable and imperfect – starting with ourselves and those around us.

See also: Appreciation; Jolliness; Love as Generosity; Splitting and Integration.

L

¶ Listening as Editing

One of the kindest, most helpful and most interesting things we can ever do with another person is to listen to them well. But good listening doesn't just involve paying attention to what someone is saying. There's a far more active side to the listening process that could properly be described as 'editing'; in key ways, it is similar to the work done for an author by an ideal literary editor.

Classically, a good editor doesn't merely accept a manuscript as it is first presented. They set about interrogating, cutting, expanding and focusing the text – not in the name of changing the fundamentals of what the author is saying, but of bringing out a range of underlying intentions that have been threatened by digressions, hesitations, losses of confidence and lapses of attention. The editor doesn't change the author into someone else; they help them to become who they really are.

The same process is at work with a good listener. They too know that some of what a speaker is saying doesn't accurately reflect what they truly mean. Perhaps they want to touch on a sensitive, sad point, but are frightened of being too heavy or of imposing. Maybe the speaker wants to pin down why something was beautiful or exciting, but get bogged down in details, repetitions or subplots. There might be an emotional truth they are trying to express, but the quality of their insight is undermined by the feeling that it would be more normal and safer to stick to factual details.

A good editorially minded listener knows how gently to correct these tendencies. They will in the kindest way possible ask the speaker to unpack their feelings more intensely and elaborate upon emotions with a sense that these will prove hugely interesting rather than boring or alarming to the audience. They help the speaker to close down stray subplots, and nudge them back to the central story, which has been lost in details. When the speaker gets tongue-tied from fear, the good editor-listener is on hand with reassurance and encouragement. They know how to signal an open mind and hint at a welcome berth for all manner of unusual-sounding but important confessions.

The good editor-listener will be responsible for a lot of changes in a conversation. Were it to be transcribed and manually edited, there would be red pencil marks everywhere across the text. But the result of such deft interventions is never a sense of violation, but an impression of having been brought closer to one's real intentions.

An ideal editor-listener helps us to be more ourselves than we know how to be by ourselves.

See also: Love as Generosity; Warmth.

¶ Loneliness

Loneliness is the fundamental condition of humankind. This fact is heavily denied by Romantic culture, which promises us that there are in fact a few people who will be able to understand us fully – a fairy tale that causes us untold difficulty.

A high degree of loneliness is an inexorable part of being a sensitive, intelligent human. It is a built-in feature of a complex existence. We must all die alone, which really means that our pain is for us alone to endure. Others can throw us words of encouragement, but in every life we are out on the ocean drowning in the swell while others, even the nice ones, stand on the shore, waving good-naturedly.

It is unlikely that we will ever find someone on exactly the same page of the soul as us: we will long for utter congruity, but there will be constant dissonance because we appeared on the earth at different times, are the product of different experiences, and are not made of quite the same fabric.

The problem is sure to get worse the more thoughtful and perceptive we are. There will simply be fewer people like us around. Acute loneliness is a specially punitive tax we have to pay to atone for a certain complexity of mind.

At an exasperated moment, near the end of his life, the German writer Goethe, who appeared to have had a lot of friends, exploded bitterly: 'No one has ever properly understood me, I have never fully understood anyone; and no one understands anyone else.'

It was a helpful outburst from a great man. It isn't our fault: a degree of distance and mutual incomprehension is not a sign that life has gone wrong; it's what we should expect from the very start. And when we do, benefits may flow. The history of art is the record of people who couldn't find anyone in the vicinity to talk to. We can take up the coded offer of intimacy in the words of a Roman poet who died in 10 BCE or the lyrics of a singer who described just our blues in a recording from Nashville in 1963.

Loneliness makes us more capable of true intimacy if better opportunities ever come along. It heightens the conversations we have with ourselves; it gives us a character. We don't repeat what everyone else thinks. We develop a point of view. We might be isolated for now, but we'll be capable of far closer, more interesting bonds with anyone we do eventually locate.

Loneliness renders us elegant and strangely alluring. It suggests there is more about us to understand than the normal patterns of social intercourse can accommodate – which is something to take pride in. A sense of isolation truly is – as we suspect but usually prevent ourselves from feeling from fear of arrogance – a sign of depth. When we admit our loneliness, we are signing up to a club that includes the people we know from the paintings of Edward Hopper, the poems of Baudelaire and the songs of Leonard Cohen.

Lonely, we enter a long and grand tradition; we find ourselves (surprisingly) in great company.

See also: Normality; Oral Sex; Psychological Asymmetry; Sane Insanity; Warmth.

¶ Long-Term Love

Much of our collective thinking about love targets the problems we face around starting a relationship. To the Romantic, love essentially means 'finding love'. What we blithely call a love story is mostly in fact the start of a love story.

Yet the true, heroic challenges of love are concerned with how to keep love going over the long term, in the face of hurdles not generally discussed in art and, as a result, lacking glamour: incompatible work schedules, differing ideas about bathroom etiquette, phone calls with ex-partners, waning lust, the demands of household management, business trips that clash with anniversaries, the question of whether and when to have children, divergent parenting styles, problematic in-laws and economic stresses.

To negotiate these challenges, long-term love requires us to develop a host of skills that our societies tend to stay quiet about: forgiveness, charity, humour, imagination and seeing the other as a loveable idiot (rather than simply a disappointment). To love over time involves striving to understand what another person is really trying to say when they are upset, even if what they are uttering is on the surface shockingly disdainful. It might involve discovering the dignity of domestic chores or a melancholy acceptance that a good relationship might require the sacrifice of certain dreams of sexual fulfilment.

We'll have to say sorry even if we are not really at fault; we'll have to tell many little white lies and occasionally rather large ones; we'll have to face the fact that we'll discover some grim shortcomings in the other person, and they in us.

Realistic, scratchy, long-term love is diametrically at odds with the Romantic vision of being in love. Therefore, by the standards of Romantic love, it has to look like an unfolding catastrophe. Far from it: it is what naturally happens when love is reciprocated and when decent, normal people live side by side for a long time. It is part of what good ordinary relationships look like over the years. It is what happens when love succeeds.

See also: *Crushes; Domesticity; Loving and Being Loved; Romantic Instinct; Sex and Love.*

¶ Lottery of Life

In the modern world, many countries have lotteries in which millions of people participate every week in the hope of suddenly acquiring a substantial fortune. A striking thing is that it's often quite disadvantaged and uneducated people who are most enthusiastic about lotteries. We might smile at their folly in getting statistics quite so wrong; if they had the wisdom and mathematical intelligence to understand how slim their chances were, they'd surely never bother. The chances of winning the largest payout is around one in fourteen million. We naturally feel a bit sorry for people investing in such slender hopes; they are taking aim at an impossibly small target.

But we're probably no better. We may not have a sense that we're playing any kind of lottery, and yet we are: the Lottery of Life. We too are clutching tickets of various kinds and setting our sights on statistical near-miracles – even while we think we're being utterly sober, rational and level-headed. The crucial place where this lottery-like behaviour happens is in relation to our hopes of happiness in two areas in particular: love and work.

If we were forced to spell out a picture of an ideally successful life, it might go something like this. We early on pick just the right area of work to apply ourselves to, swerve neatly into new fields at the ideal moment, and receive public recognition, money and honour for our efforts. Work is fun, creative and utterly in line with our talents.

There are similar satisfactions to be had around love. After a spate of compelling and passionate relationships, we meet one very special, beautiful, kind and devoted person who understands us completely – often without us needing to communicate with words. Sex is extraordinary and children and domesticity never grind us down. We enjoy perfect health and retire with the feeling of having accomplished what we set out to do. We experience a dignified, respected old age, admired by our descendants and occasionally exercising a deft guiding touch behind the scenes as an *éminence grise*. We die gently in our late nineties of a non-painful illness in a tranquil, flower-filled room, having written a wise and generous will.

Such scenarios occur about as often as a payout on the lottery. But (to our surprise, despite our education and apparently realistic and practical natures), we may have strongly invested in some modified version of just this form of phantasm. We don't grasp just how rare and strange ninety years on earth without calamities in love and work might actually be.

If we could see what love and work were really like for most other people, we'd be much less sad about our own situation and attainments. If we could fly across the world and peer into everyone's lives and minds like an all-seeing angel, we'd perceive how very frequent disappointment is, how much unfulfilled ambition is circulating, how much confusion and uncertainty is played out in private, and how many break-downs and intemperate arguments unfold with every new day. Then we would realise just how abnormal – statistically speaking – and therefore cruel the goals we have set ourselves really are.

It would be a painful lesson in some ways. We might be shocked and saddened by what we saw. We would be disappointed, of course, to conclude that, in all probability, we wouldn't achieve what we'd hoped for. But in another way it would be a comforting and deeply reassuring experience. We'd feel a little more tenderness towards ourselves for not having – in effect – won the Lottery of Life.

Without being overtly naive, most of us are holding out hopes equivalent to thinking we might win a major lottery. We don't deserve criticism. We need to pity ourselves for the formidable obstacles that stand in the way of the kind of success that it is so normal to want, yet so rare to have.

See also: Expectations; Luck; Meritocracy; Normality.

¶ Love as Education

At the heart of the Romantic vision of love is an idea of complete mutual acceptance. To seek to change one's lover feels like a profound offence against the whole idea of love.

This way of thinking about and experiencing love can feel entirely natural, but it is a relatively recent historical invention. It stands in sharp contrast to a much older and in certain ways wiser view: the Classical idea that love is an arena of growth and change. This view of love was developed in Ancient Greece, prompted particularly by the philosophical ideas of Socrates and Plato. As they saw it, the task of love is first and foremost to educate one's lover. We don't love someone because we think they are perfect already, but because we can see what they could be; we love their potential and their emergent (but not yet fully developed) qualities. Their deep attachment to us means that we have an ideal opportunity for guiding and shaping their development towards the articulation of their full potential. Love is a mutually supportive structure in which two people can guide one another to their respective virtuous ideal selves.

This pedagogical view of love now sounds extremely odd. We don't imagine love as a classroom. Our current culture imagines the lover as a great admirer. Classical culture imagined them as a great teacher – the person best fitted to edge us towards becoming who we should be. We are suspicious because we think of teaching in the guise of nagging: the pure demand for change, rather than an eloquent enticement to surrender our entrenched flaws.

See also: Love Me as I Am; Teaching and Learning.

¶ Love as Generosity

To fall in love with someone is typically assumed to involve awe at a person's physical and psychological virtues. We think of ourselves as 'in love' when we are bewitched by a rare creature who seems in myriad ways stronger and more accomplished than we are; our love seems founded on admiration.

But there is another view of love that deserves to be explored; a philosophy of love founded on generosity. From this perspective, to love means not only or primarily to experience admiration in the face of perfection; it involves a capacity to be uncommonly generous towards a fellow human at moments when they may be less than straightforwardly appealing. Love is taken to mean not a thrill in the face of accomplishment but a distinctive skill founded on the ability to see beyond a person's off-putting outer dimensions, an energy to enter imaginatively into their experiences and bestow an ongoing degree of forgiveness and kindness in spite of marked trickiness and confusion.

See also: Being 'Good'; Crushes; Emotional Translation; Kintsugi; Listening as Editing; Loving and Being Loved; Romantic Disappointment; Snobbery; Universal Love; Weakness of Strength.

¶ Love Me as I Am

Our culture strongly inclines us to the view that genuine love must involve complete acceptance of another person in their good and especially somewhat bad sides. In moments of fury with our partners, we may be tempted to dismiss their complaints against us with the cry: 'Love me as I am'.

But in truth, none of us should want to remain exactly as we are – and therefore none of us should too strongly want another person to love (as opposed to tolerate or simply forgive) what is warped within us.

Genuine love might be defined as gently and kindly helping someone to become the best version of themselves rather than accepting them precisely as they are. It isn't a betrayal of love for someone to try to help us evolve or to teach us to be better people; it may be the highest proof of genuine commitment.

Unfortunately, under the sway of Romantic ideology that makes us suspicious of emotional education, most of us end up being terrible teachers and equally terrible students. We don't accept the legitimacy, let alone nobility, of others' desire to teach us and can't acknowledge areas where we might need to be taught. We rebel against the very structure of a lover's education that would enable criticism to be moulded into sensible-sounding lessons and to be heard as caring attempts to rejig the more troublesome aspects of our personalities.

At the first sign that the other is adopting a teacherly tone, we tend to assume that we are being 'attacked' and betrayed. We therefore close our ears to the instruction, reacting with sarcasm and aggression to the teacher.

Our stance is deeply understandable: to the mother, everything about the tiny infant is delightful; they wouldn't change even the smallest thing; their baby is perfect just as it is. Our idea of love has taken this attitude to heart: it's what (we think) love is supposed to be like. The suggestion that another could change, grow, or improve is taken as an insult to love.

The problem is: the mother never in fact loved us just as we were. She hoped we would keep growing up. And the need is still there. Our bodies may be fully formed, but our psyches always have some way to go. We shouldn't hold it against our lovers if they don't love us as we are, if they'd sweetly like us to be a bit different.

See also: Love as Education; Teaching and Learning.

¶ Loving and Being Loved

Curiously, we speak of love as one thing rather than discerning the two very different varieties that lie beneath a single word: being loved and loving. It appears that we can only make a relationship work properly when we are ready to do the latter and are aware of our unnatural, immature fixation on the former.

We start knowing only about being loved. It comes to seem very wrongly like the norm. To the child, it feels as if the parent is simply spontaneously on hand to comfort, guide, entertain, feed and clear up while remaining almost always warm and cheerful. The parents don't reveal how often they've bitten their tongue, fought back tears, and been too tired to take off their clothes after a day of childcare.

We learn of love in an entirely non-reciprocal context. The parent loves but they don't expect the favour to be returned in any significant way. The parent doesn't get upset when the child doesn't notice a new haircut or ask carefully calibrated questions about how the meeting at work went or suggest that the parent go upstairs and take a much-needed nap. Parent and child may both love, but each party is on a very different end of the axis -- unbeknownst to the child.

This is why in adulthood when we first say that we long for love, what we predominantly mean is that we want to be loved as we were once loved by a parent. We want a re-creation in adulthood of what it felt like to be administered to and indulged. In a secret part of our minds, we picture someone who will understand our needs, bring us what we want, be immensely sympathetic and patient towards us, act selflessly and make many things better.

Naturally, this is a disaster for our unions. For any relationship to work, we need to move firmly out of the position of the child and into that of the parent. We need to become someone who can sometimes subordinate their own demands to the needs of another.

To be adults in love, we have to learn – perhaps for the very first time – to do something truly remarkable: to put someone else ahead of us, for a time at least. That's what true, mature love actually is, much to everyone's initial surprise.

See also: Long-Term Love; Love as Generosity; Other-as-Child; Romantic Disappointment.

¶ Luck

Nowadays, we don't much believe in luck – or what in earlier ages was known as Fortune. We would think it extremely suspicious if someone explained that they had been sacked, but added that this was simply the result of 'bad luck'. We would think it equally strange if someone said they had made many millions, but ascribed their triumph to mere 'good luck'. We resist the notion that luck can play a significant role as much in our failures as in our successes. Luck presents a substantial offence against modern ideals of control, strategy and foresight. We understand ourselves to be – for better and for worse – the authors of our own destinies.

Modern civilisation itself could be viewed as a gigantic protest against the role of chance in human affairs. Science, insurance, medicine and public education take up arms against luck, and have won enormous battles against it; so many, in fact, that it has grown devilishly tempting to believe that we may have vanquished chance altogether.

However, luck is a fearsome enemy; its territory is fluid and its power unpredictable and tempestuous. Wisdom requires us to accept that it will never be entirely tamed. Within every success, however ardent our efforts, there is sure to be a substantial degree of luck. More redemptively, within every failure there is sure to be much that cannot be ascribed to our foolishness alone. We make small mistakes all the time; it is only occasionally that a modest error turns out to have devastating consequences.

There are some who already believe too much in luck; they are excessively willing to assign all the outcomes of their lives to chance. They need to hear more about responsibility and the capacity of individuals to transform their circumstances. But, in many ways, these passive actors are ever less common in the modern world. For the rest of us, those who operate with a daunting feeling of personal responsibility, who will constantly push themselves to match their highest expectations and berate themselves for failure, a reverential belief in luck should be far more than a historical curiosity. It remains a crucial concept to take the edge off our arrogance and, when fate has turned against us, to temper the violence of our self-contempt.

See also: Day of Judgement; Expectations; Lottery of Life; Meritocracy; Suicide; Tragedy.

¶ Meaning of Life, The

A meaningful life is close to, but at points importantly different from, a happy life. A meaningful life draws upon, and exercises, a range of our higher capacities: those bound up with tenderness, care, connection, self-understanding, sympathy, intelligence and creativity.

A meaningful life aims not so much at day-to-day contentment as fulfilment. We may be leading a meaningful life and yet often be in a bad mood – just as we may be having frequent surface fun while living, for the most part, meaninglessly.

A meaningful life is bound up with the long term. Projects, relationships, interests and commitments will build up cumulatively. Meaningful activities leave something behind, even when the emotions that once propelled us into them have passed.

Meaningful activities aren't necessarily those we do most often. They are those we value most highly and will, from the perspective of our deaths, regret most deeply.

The question of what makes life meaningful has to be answered personally, even if our conclusions are marked by no particular idiosyncrasy. Others cannot be relied upon to determine what will be meaningful to us. What we call 'crises of meaning' are generally moments when someone else's – perhaps well-intentioned – interpretation of what might be meaningful to us runs up against a growing realisation of our divergent tastes and interests.

By a process of experience and introspection, we have to work out what counts as meaningful in our eyes. Whereas pleasure manifests itself immediately, our taste in meaning may be more elusive. We can be relatively far into our lives before we securely identify what lends them their meaning.

That said, The School of Life considers that meaningful lives are generally anchored around eight themes: love, family, work, friendship, culture, politics, nature and philosophy. Most are well known; the point isn't to identify entirely new sources of meaning so much as to try to evoke and explain some familiar choices.

M

To wonder too openly, or intensely, about the Meaning of Life sounds like a peculiar, ill-fated and unintentionally comedic pastime. It isn't anything an ordinary mortal should be doing – or would get very far by doing. Without always acknowledging it, we are operating with a remarkably ungenerous perspective on the Meaning of Life.

Yet the subject is for everyone; it is for all of us to wonder about, and define, a meaningful existence. There need be nothing forbidding about the issue. A meaningful life can be simple in structure, personal, usable, attractive and familiar. It is time to turn the pursuit of a meaningful life from a comedically complex impossibility to something we can all comprehend, aim for and succeed at.

See also: Eudaimonia

¶ Meaningful Work

When we talk about jobs being meaningful or meaningless, we are at heart asking whether these jobs are helping anyone's life to be better: we're wondering whether our work stands a chance of increasing someone's pleasure or reducing their suffering. Unlike what standard economics tells us, we are desperate to make a significant contribution to the good. It is hard to be happy at work without a sense that we have proved of assistance to someone else.

One of the greatest enemies of 'meaning' in the modern world is the sheer scale of businesses. Corporations coordinate the labours of tens, even hundreds, of thousands of people – and raise productivity exponentially. But extreme specialisation and global reach can gravely reduce the sense of meaning that any one employee might have. A packaging supervisor in Malmö might not have much idea of how their work fits in with the activities of a geochemist in Ghana who compares activated alumina with indigenous laterite and bauxite as potential sorbents for removing fluoride from drinking water, or with the concerns of a legal expert currently staying in the Alvear Hotel in Buenos Aires and reporting to a steering committee in New York about the implications of proposed revisions to Section 14 of the Argentine Mining Code. All these individuals might be working for the same rather noble cause, but none of them can quite remember day to day what the real cause actually is.

Most work now takes place within gigantic organisations that are engaged in a variety of large, complicated and slow-moving projects. Therefore it can be hard to derive, on a daily basis, any tangible sense of having improved anyone else's life. The customer and the end product are, in the gigantic structures of modernity, simply too far away in space and too distant in time. One can be unable easily to reassure oneself of one's worth and purpose when one is only a single unit among a twenty-thousand-strong team on four continents pushing forward a project that might be ready in five years' time.

There are sound reasons why the work practices of large organisations proceed at such scale – typically at a glacial pace. Product developments in aeronautics and banking, oil and pharmaceuticals cannot happen overnight. The timeframes are logical, but in terms of individual experience, they go directly against our natural, deeply embedded preference for a rapidly unfolding story.

The Ancient Greek philosopher Aristotle observed that a key requirement for a satisfying piece of theatre was that it should be over relatively quickly. There might be tensions and complications and unexpected changes of direction, but in a few hours and three acts, there should be a feeling of genuine completion. It's not just in the theatre that speed is attractive. The concentration of action also helps to explain the appeal of sport. In ninety minutes, a football match can take us from a perfect, neutral start to a precise result.

However, if football were like modern work in terms of scale and pace, one can imagine it unfolding on eighteen pitches with twenty-two balls and two thousand players kicking around for thousands of days without any overview of the progress of the game. By the standards of our innate longings, our work unfolds in a very disordered, over-extended and confusing way.

Our labour feels meaningful not only when it is fast, but also when we get to witness the ways we are helping others: when we can leave the office, factory or shop with an impression of having fixed a problem in someone else's life. This pleasure too is threatened by scale. In the massive organisations of modernity, we may be so distant from the end users of our products and services as to be unable to derive any real benefit from our constructive role in their lives. Spending days improving terms on contracts in the logistics industry truly will lead to a moment when a couple can contentedly enjoy

M

some ginger biscuits together in front of the TV; optimising data management across different parts of an aerospace firm truly will – along with thousands of other coordinated efforts – contribute to the moment when a young family can bond together on a beach holiday. The connections are genuine, but they are so extended and convoluted as to feel dispiritingly flimsy and unreal in our minds.

It is a tantalising paradox, and a kind of tragedy, that because of the unavoidable scale of modern work, we may pass our lives helping other people and yet, day to day, be burdened by a harrowing feeling of having made no difference whatsoever.

Part of the answer to our feelings of disconnection and disorientation lies in a discipline at the heart of culture: the art of storytelling. As the complexity and scale of organisations increase, so we need to learn how to arrange a disparate selection of events into a master narrative that can lend them coherence and thereby remind us of how we might fit into a meaningful whole. A company's 'story' has a lot in common with a large, layered novel. One can imagine a company novel that would begin with a description of someone accessing a bank account in Salzburg. The next moment, we would be in a restaurant in the Wan Chai district of Hong Kong, where a deal is being hammered out to transfer crates to Dubai. Then the focus would be on a meeting taking place in a basement in Whitehall, where regulations for consumer goods would be discussed between ministers and a set of civil servants. Then would come a section set in a call centre in Phoenix, closely followed by a scene in a nursery in Seattle. But rather than a hopeless confusion, the point would be to reveal how these apparently random incidents were in fact profoundly interconnected, pointing to a grand synthetic goal: the creation of a new IT system for an office in Munich, or a project to increase the flow rate of a pump production line in southern Spain.

Once scattered events are woven together into a story, they can start to feel very meaningful indeed. Ideally, every large company would have storytellers on the payroll.

See also: Duty Trap, The; Service; Specialisation; Vocation Myth; Work/Life Balance.

¶ Melancholy

Melancholy is not rage or bitterness; it is a noble species of sadness that arises when we are open to the fact that life is inherently difficult for everyone and that suffering and disappointment are at the heart of human experience. It is not a disorder that needs to be cured; it is a tender-hearted, calm, dispassionate acknowledgement of how much pain we must all inevitably travel through.

Modern society tends to emphasise buoyancy and cheerfulness. It is impatient with melancholy states, and wishes either to medicalise – and therefore 'solve' – them, or deny their legitimacy altogether.

Melancholy links pain with wisdom and beauty. It springs from a rightful awareness of the tragic structure of every life. In melancholy states, we can understand without fury or sentimentality that no one truly understands anyone else, that loneliness is universal, and that every life has its full measure of shame and sorrow. The melancholy know that many of the things we most want are in tragic conflict: to feel secure, and yet to be free; to have money and yet not to have to be beholden to others; to be in close-knit communities and yet not to be stifled by the expectations and demands of society; to travel and explore the world and yet to put down deep roots; to fulfil the demands of our appetites for food, exploration and sloth – and yet stay thin, sober, faithful and fit.

M

The wisdom of the melancholy attitude (as opposed to the bitter or angry one) lies in the understanding that we have not been singled out; that our suffering belongs to humanity in general. Melancholy is marked by an impersonal take on suffering. It is filled with pity for the human condition.

There are melancholy landscapes and melancholy pieces of music, melancholy poems and melancholy times of day. In them, we find echoes of our own griefs, returned back to us without some of the personal associations that, when they first struck us, made them particularly agonising.

The task of culture is to turn both rage and its disguised twin, jolliness, into melancholy.

The more melancholy a culture can be, the less its individual members need to be persecuted by their own failures, lost illusions and regrets.

When it can be shared, melancholy is the beginning of friendship.

See also: Consolation; Jolliness; Splitting and Integration; Vulnerability.

¶ Memento Mori

In theory, we know we're going to die. But there is a huge difference between an intellectual knowledge of the fact and a direct sensory realisation. The oversight costs us dear, for it is only through a visceral awareness of our impending end that we are granted the courage and urgency to get on with the vital (but often daunting) tasks of our lives.

The Renaissance artistic tradition of the Memento Mori ('Reminder of death') provided striking visual images to keep the idea of our own mortality and the radically uncertain time of our demise constantly before our eyes. The theorists of this tradition grasped that for an idea to be compelling and to guide our conduct with true force, it needs to come via art – that is, wrapped up in a seductive outer layer that appeals to our emotions. We need to see a haunting skull, weeping mourners, rotting flesh, so that what might otherwise have been merely abstract and easily dismissed can turn into a resonant truth with a chance of truly influencing how we live.

The Memento Mori is an example of art being used for a precise psychological purpose. Instead of waiting for artists to produce whatever happened to interest them, the philosophers of the Renaissance identified important needs and commissioned artists to work on them. Painters were given a specific job description: makers of things that remind us of death. Ideas were united with the tools for their powerful transmission.

Such a psychological mission should remain a central purpose of artistic activity. The task of art is to find new and freshly forceful ways of keeping the most important ideas about how to live and die well constantly at the front of our minds.

See also: Akrasia, Art, The Purpose of; Ritual, Seduction.

M

¶ Meritocracy

A meritocracy is a society in which money, jobs and honour are handed out on the basis of talent and merit rather than birth or personal contacts.

The modern world is widely assumed to be moving in an ever more meritocratic direction. It is applauded for doing so, and condemned for not doing so fast enough.

But there is a darker side to the idea of meritocracy: if we truly believe that we have created (or could one day create) a world where the successful truly merited all their success, it follows that we have to hold the failures exclusively responsible for their failures. In a meritocratic age, an element of justice enters into the distribution of wealth, but also of poverty. Low status comes to seem not merely regrettable but also deserved.

The question of why, if one is in any way good, clever or able, one is still poor becomes infinitely more acute and painful for the unsuccessful to have to answer (to themselves and others) in a new meritocratic age.

Meritocracy turns failure from a problem into a catastrophe.

See also: Day of Judgement; Equality and Envy; Lottery of Life; Luck; Snobbery; Suicide

¶ Misemployment

Employment refers to the state of being generically in work. Misemployment refers to the state of being in work but of a kind that fails to tackle with any sincerity the higher needs of others, merely exciting them to unsatisfactory desires and pleasures instead.

The ranks of the misemployed are populated by workers who make cigarettes, addictive but sterile television shows, badly designed condos, ill-fitting and shoddy clothes, deceptive advertisements, artery-clogging biscuits, and tempting but highly sugared drinks.

The rate of Misemployment in the economy is never formally measured, but it might be very high. In the Utopia, government would track not just how many people had a job, but how many had a job that catered to higher needs. Economists have, with moderate success, been learning techniques to reduce the overall rate of unemployment. Central to their strategy is the lowering of interest rates and the printing of money. In the language of the field, the key to bringing down unemployment is to 'stimulate demand'. Although technically effective, this method fails to draw any distinction between good and bad demand and therefore between employment and Misemployment.

There are real solutions to bringing down the rate of Misemployment. The trick isn't just to stimulate demand per se but to stimulate good demand: to excite people to buy the constituents of true satisfaction, and therefore to give individuals and businesses a chance to direct their labour, and make profits, in meaningful areas of the economy.

In a nation properly concerned with Misemployment, the taste of the audience would be educated to demand and pay for the most important things. Twenty per cent of the adult population might therefore be employed in mental health and flourishing. At least another thirty per cent would be employed in building an environment that could satisfy the soul.

To achieve such a state, it isn't enough to print money. The task is to excite people to want to spend it on the right things. This requires public education so that audiences will recognise the importance of what is truly valuable and walk past what betrays their potential.

M

Employment figures are far from irrelevant; they matter a great deal. They are the first things that need to be attended to. All the same, the raw figures mask a more ambitious goal: that of learning to deploy human capital in a properly admirable way.

See also: Architecture; Faulty Walnut, The; Secularisation; Utopia.

¶ Monasteries

Today we probably think of monasteries as distant, rather grand and beautiful reminders of the Middle Ages – as far removed from any of the concerns of our modern lives as it is possible to get.

However, in their heyday, monasteries were doing something that retains a universal relevance even for those of a secular disposition. They were highly engineered machines for helping their inhabitants to think. They were begun because certain people wanted to think very carefully about a range of vital questions: what is the nature of God and what does God want from me? What is the Divine and what is Grace? What is owed to Jesus and what is owed to Caesar?

These believers realised that the human mind is an extremely flighty and easily distracted organ. The prospect of a party at the end of the week, the chatter of a few people out in the street, the sight of an exciting book – all these can derail our attempts to focus our minds.

So the founders of monasteries went to immense efforts to create environments that could positively assist their members to think fruitfully. They situated their buildings far from cities; they built high walls around their estates; they laid out highly symmetrical gardens and walkways; they made sure their food was nutritious but plain. They encouraged only quiet conversation over meals. They went to bed early and rose at dawn. They did moderate exercise every other day.

Today, we probably don't want to think so much about the particular questions that monks and nuns once focused on. However, we still have a lot of thinking to do. We have equally important thinking tasks to perform around relationships, work and the meaning of our lives.

For these challenges, monasteries retain some important lessons for us. We can be inspired by their ambition to go beyond ordinary expectations and set up ideal conditions where a person might think as well as possible. This contrasts with a more Romantic attitude that sees thinking as mainly influenced by other thoughts – particularly by books – and doesn't quite accept that an organ as elevated as the mind may be assisted by something as ostensibly trivial as going for a walk or having only a light salad for lunch.

In the Utopia, we should learn to design our own highly engineered machines for thinking – institutions geared to the task of deftly extracting our best thoughts from our squeamish and recalcitrant minds.

See also: *Addiction; Architecture; Faulty Walnut, The; Secularisation; Utopia.*

¶ Music

Music is of central importance to most of us. Tellingly, we are extremely picky not just about what music we listen to, but also about when we do so. To understand why, we need to focus on a peculiar but crucial fact about ourselves. We are highly emotional beings, but not all of our emotions make their way fully and properly to the front of our conscious attention when they need to. They are there, but only in a latent, muted, undeveloped way. There's too much noise both externally and internally.

M

In the background, we may be storing up the ingredients for a range of profound and potentially very important emotions: the raw matter for grief or sorrow; a sense of tender generosity towards humanity in general; a quiet sense of the beauty of modesty; or pity for ourselves. We may ponder all the errors we didn't mean to make; all the ways we've wasted our potential or didn't properly return love when it was offered. These feelings and many others are the emotional containers of profound wisdom. But they may not have the sway they ideally should in our lives because they don't get sustained attention and an opportunity to develop. They exist as confused, weak signals in us – hardly noticeable, easily disregarded blips of sensation, raw matter that has not been catalysed. The beauty, goodness, consolation and strength they could bring us never quite emerge; we bear within us a legacy of unfelt feelings.

This is why music matters: it offers amplification and encouragement. Specific pieces of music give strength and support to valuable but tentative emotional dispositions. A euphoric song amplifies the faint but ecstatic feeling that we could love everyone and find true delight in being alive. Day to day, these feelings exist, but are buried by the pressure to be limited, cautious and reserved. The song pushes them forward and gives them confidence; it provides the space in which they can grow. Given this encouragement, we can give them a bigger place in our lives.

A sombre, tender piece may coax to the surface our submerged sadness. Under its encouraging tutelage, we can more easily feel sorry for the ways we have hurt others; we can pay greater attention to our own inner pain (and hence be more appreciative of small acts of gentleness from others); we become more alive to universal suffering, to the fact that everyone loses the things they love, and that everyone is burdened with regrets. With the help of particular chords, a compassionate side of ourselves, which is normally hard to access, becomes more prominent.

A different kind of music might take up our low-key impulses to action and self-transformation: it rouses us; it quickens our pace. We want to stride to its beat and make the best use of our energies while there is still time. Other songs could boost our fragile sense that certain things don't really matter all that much. The meeting didn't go very well, but so what? In the end it's not that important. The kitchen was a bit messy, but it's not a big deal in the cosmic scheme. Our reserves of perspective are activated; we are fortified in our capacity to cope with the petty irritations that would otherwise undermine us.

Like an amplifier with its signal, music doesn't invent emotion; it takes what is there and makes it louder. One might worry that boosting an emotion might be risky. After all, not everything we feel is worthy of encouragement. It is possible to use music to magnify feelings of hatred or to inflate violent impulses; the culture ministries of fascist dictatorships have been fatefully skilled at doing just this. But, almost always, we face a very different issue around music: we're not building up our courage to lay waste to civilisation. We want to strengthen our capacities for calm, forgiveness, love and appreciation.

In our relationship to music we're seeking the right soundtrack for our lives. A soundtrack in a film helps accord the due emotional resonance to a specific scene. It helps us register the actual pathos of a situation that might be missed if we relied on words and images alone; it helps us fully recognise the identity of a moment.

Exactly the same is true in our lives: we're constantly faced with situations where something significant is going on; at the back of our minds the helpful emotional reaction is there, but it's subdued and drowned out by the ambient noise of existence. Music is the opposite of noise: it is the cure for noise. By finding the right piece of music at the right time we're adding an accompanying score that highlights the emotions we should be feeling more strongly and allows our own best reactions to be more prominent and secure. We end up feeling the emotions that are our due.

See also: Art, The Purpose of; Artistic Rebalancing.

N

¶ Nagging

Nagging is the dispiriting, unpleasant, counter-productive but wholly understandable and poignant version of a hugely noble ambition: the desire to change other people.

There is so much we might fairly want to change about people. We want them to be more self-aware, punctual, generous, reliable, introspective, resilient, communicative and profound. At home, we want them to focus more on the sink, the children, the bins, the money and the need to put the phone down and look up. At a macro dimension, we want them to think more about the suffering of encaged animals, the destruction of our habitat and the iniquities of capitalism. The desire to change people is no pathology; it is a clear-sighted recognition of the scale of human wickedness.

In its essence, nagging is an attempt at teaching, at transmitting an idea for improvement from one mind into another. But it is also a version of teaching that has given up hope. It has descended into an attempt to insist rather than invite, to coerce rather than charm. One has grown too weary and humiliated by constant rebuffs to have the energy to seduce. One is too panicked by the thought that the unteachable 'student' is ruining one's life to find the inner resources to see it a little more from their point of view. It is one's own suffering that dominates all the available imaginative capacity.

So one gets straight to the point, gets rid of the garlands, omits the honey and says it in plain terms. The bins need attention now. Get to the table immediately. You're a selfish layabout. Not there, here... One isn't wrong. One is very right, but also very tired and, deep down, grief-stricken.

Lamentably, also, it doesn't work. By the time one has started humiliating any student, the lesson is over. Nagging breeds its evil twin, shirking. The other pretends to read the paper, goes upstairs and feels righteous. The shrillness of one's tone gives them all the excuse they need to trust that we have nothing kind or true to tell them.

One changes others only when the desire that they evolve has not reached an insistent pitch; when we can still bear that they remain as they are. All of us improve only when we have not been badgered or made to feel guilty; only when we have a sense that we are loved and deeply understood for the many reasons why change is so hard for us. We know, of course, that the bins need our attention, that we should strive to get to bed earlier and that we have been a disappointment. But we can't bear to hear these lessons in an unsympathetic tone; tricky children that we are, we want to be indulged for our ambivalence about becoming better people.

The same obtuse dynamic is at play at the political level. We know we shouldn't abuse the planet, bend rules or close our hearts to the unfortunate. But we won't do any of the good things if a dour figure wags their finger and delivers stern lectures. We want to be charmed, not dragged, into goodness.

The tragedy of nagging is that its causes are usually so noble, and still it doesn't work. We nag because we feel that our possession of the truth lets us off having to convey it elegantly. It never does. The solution to nagging is not to give up trying to get others to do what we want. Rather, it is to recognise that persuasion needs to occur in terms that make sense to those we want to alter.

See also: Artistic Sympathy; Saints; Seduction; Teaching and Learning.

¶ Nastiness

It happens pretty much all the time: a small jabbing comment, a joke at our expense amid a group of old friends, a line of sarcasm, a sneering assessment, a provocative comment on the internet.

These things hurt a lot – more than we're ever allowed to admit. In the privacy of our minds, we search for explanations, but anything satisfying and soothing is usually hard to come by. We're left to puzzle at the casual inhumanity that circulates all around us – and suspect that, somewhere deep down, it's we who are to blame for falling victim to it.

This is what we should actually think, a truth as basic as it is inviolable: other people have been nasty because they are in pain. The only reason they have hurt us is because, somewhere deep inside, they are hurting themselves. They have been catty, derogatory and foul because they are not well. However outwardly confident they may look, however virile and robust they may appear, their actions are all the evidence we need that they cannot be in a good place. No one solid would ever need to do this.

The thought is empowering because nastiness so readily humiliates and reduces us. It turns us into the small damaged party. Without meaning to, we begin to imagine our bully as potent and even somehow impressive. Their vindictiveness demeans us. But the psychological explanation of evil at once reverses the power dynamic. It is you, who has no need to belittle, who is in fact the larger, steelier, more forceful party; you – who feels so defenceless – who is actually in power.

The thought restores justice. It promises that the guilty party has – after all – been punished along the way. You might not have been able to right the scales personally, but a kind of punishment has been delivered cosmically somewhere behind the scenes; their suffering, of which their need to inflict suffering on others is incontrovertible evidence, is all you need to know that they have been served their just desserts. You move from being a victim of crime to being an audience to an abstract form of justice. They may not be apologising to you, but they haven't escaped freely either; their sulphur is proof that they are paying a heavy price.

This is not merely a pleasant story. A person who feels at ease with themselves can have no need to distress others. We don't have the energy to be cruel unless, and until, we are in inner torment.

Along the way, the theory hints at how we might – when we have recovered from the blow – deal with those who dealt it. The temptation is to be stern and cruel back, but the only way to diminish the vicious cycle of hate is to address its origins, which lie in suffering. There is no point punching back. We must learn to look upon our enemies with sorrow, pity and, when we can manage it, a forgiving kind of love.

See also: Androcles and the Lion.

¶ Nature

Nature is valuable not only for itself; it is also to be revered as the single most persuasive and redemptive work of philosophy.

Nature corrects our erroneous, and ultimately very painful, sense that we are essentially free. The idea that we have the freedom to fashion our own destinies as we please has become central to our contemporary worldview: we are encouraged to imagine that we can, with time, create exactly the lives we desire, around our relationships, our work and our existence more generally. This hopeful scenario has been the source of extraordinary and unnecessary suffering.

There are many things we desperately want to avoid, which we will spend huge parts of our lives worrying about and that we will then bitterly resent when they force themselves upon us nevertheless.

The idea of inevitability is central to the natural world: the deciduous tree has to shed its leaves when the temperature dips in autumn; the river must erode its banks; the cold front will deposit its rain; the tide has to rise and fall. The laws of nature are governed by forces nobody chose, no one can resist, and that brook no exception.

When we contemplate nature (a forest in the autumn, for example, or the reproductive cycle of a salmon), we are witnessing rules that in their broad irresistible structure apply to ourselves as well. We too must mature, seek to reproduce, age, fall ill and die. We face a litany of other burdens too: we will never be fully understood by others; we will always be burdened by primordial anxiety; we will never fully know what it is like to be someone else; we will invariably fantasise about more than we can have; we will realise that in key ways we cannot be who we want to be.

What we most fear will happen irrespective of our wishes. But when we see frustration as a law of nature, we drain it of some of its sting and bitterness. We recognise that limitations are not in any way unique to us. In awesome, majestic scenes (the life cycle of an elephant; the eruption of a volcano), nature moves us away from our habitual tendency to personalise and rail against our suffering.

A central task of culture should be to remind us that the laws of nature apply to us as well as to trees, clouds and cliff faces. Our goal is to become clearer about where our own tantalisingly powerful yet always limited agency stops, and where we will be left with no option but to bow to forces infinitely greater than our own.

See also: Animals; Sublime, The.

¶ News

It doesn't come with any instructions, because it's meant to be the most normal, easy, obvious and unremarkable activity in the world, like breathing or blinking. After an interval, usually no longer than a night (and often far less; if we're feeling particularly restless, we might only manage to go for five minutes before our resolve breaks), we interrupt whatever we are doing in order to check the news. We put our lives on hold in the expectation of receiving yet another dose of critical information about all the most significant achievements, catastrophes, crimes, epidemics and romantic complications to have befallen humankind around the planet since we last had a look.

Societies become modern, the philosopher Hegel suggested, when news replaces religion as our central source of guidance and our touchstone of moral authority. In the developed economies, the news now occupies a position of power at least equal to that formerly enjoyed by the faiths. News dispatches track the canonical hours with uncanny precision: matins have been transubstantiated into the breakfast bulletin, vespers into the evening report. But the news doesn't just follow a quasi-religious timetable. It also demands of us that we approach it with some of the same deferential expectations we would once have harboured of our faiths. Here, too, we hope to receive revelations, learn who is good and bad, fathom suffering and understand the unfolding logic of existence. Here too, if we refuse to take part in the rituals, there could be imputations of heresy.

For most of history, 'news' was for the few. It comprised hugely expensive information designed to help kings and queens manage their lands. There was a practical purpose behind the need to know.

Today, news is still sold to us on the basis that it is information vital for our lives. The presumption is that we need to

N

know a great deal about disasters pretty much anywhere in the world, about the doings of the rich and famous and about what's been going on in the last few hours at the top levels of government. In consequence, we get a chaotic and deeply distorted picture of a world composed of crises, violence and celebrity parties – and we are continuously pulled away from our own priorities and attempts to focus on the management of our lives.

In the Utopia, news would be much more ambitious. Outlets would compete to provide the information we needed to help us to live and die well, but didn't yet possess. This might include bulletins on what had just happened or it might include things that had happened long ago. These would be defined as 'news' because the story hadn't yet reached our ears. We might not have heard that Socrates had unravelled the mystery of love or that Emile Durkheim had worked out why we get more stressed as societies become more prosperous – even though these discoveries were made long ago – just as the invention of writing would have been 'news' to a Pictish warrior many centuries after it was common knowledge to the bureaucrats of Mesopotamia.

To succeed commercially, truly helpful news needs to be seductive, artful and entertaining; it can't just be earnest. In the ideal future, news might still have a tabloid style – attention-grabbing, brief, entertaining and making an undisguised appeal to our sensual appetites – only this style would be in the service of a more accurate assessment of what we actually need to know in order to be wise.

See also: Art and News; Censorship; History.

¶ News from Within

To lay claim to any respectability or competence, we know that we must keep up with the news. That's why we've ringed the earth with satellites, crisscrossed it with fibre-optic cables, and created networks of bureaus that inform us with maniacal urgency of pretty much any event to have unfolded anywhere on the planet in the last few moments. Furthermore, we are equipped with tiny devices that we keep very close to hand, so as to monitor all unfolding stories in close to real time. We have been granted a ringside seat on the second-by-second flow of history.

As a result, we see a lot more. At the same time, strangely, we see a lot less. The constant presence of news from without hampers our ability to pick up on an equally important, though far less prestigious, source of News from Within. We are not, by nature, well equipped to see inside ourselves. Consciousness bobs like a small boat on a sea of disavowed emotions. A lot of feelings and ideas require a high degree of courage to confront. They threaten to make us uncomfortably anxious, excited or sad were we to learn more about them.

So we use the news from without to silence the News from Within. We have the most prestigious excuse ever invented not to spend too much time roaming freely inside our own minds. It is not that the news from without is unimportant to someone – it will be the most important thing in certain people's lives a continent away, or in a company in the capital, or somewhere in the upper reaches of government. It's just that this news is almost certainly disconnected from our real priority over the coming years, which is to make the most of our life and our talents in the time that remains to us. It is touching that we should give so much of our curiosity over to strangers, but it is poignant that we are forced eventually to pay such a high price for this constant dispersal of energy. We dismiss fragile, tentative thoughts about what we should do next, who we should call, what we really need to do – thoughts

N

upon which an adequate future for us depends – for the sake of the more obvious drama of the moment. But the drama won't save us, and cares not a jot about our development or our real responsibilities.

It feels counter-intuitive to think that there might be certain things more important than the news. But there is: our own lives, which we have (troublingly) been granted such prestigious reasons and means to avoid confronting.

See also: Addiction; Philosophical Meditation

¶ Normality

Most of us are rather interested in being normal. We want to belong, and worry about ways in which we don't. No matter how much we praise individualism and celebrate ourselves as unique, we are, in many areas, deeply concerned with fitting in.

It is therefore unfortunate that our picture of what is normal is very often way out of line with what is actually true and widespread. Many things that we might assume to be uniquely odd or disconcertingly strange about us are in reality completely average and ubiquitous, though rarely spoken of in the reserved and cautious public sphere.

The idea of the normal currently in circulation is not an accurate map of what is actually customary for a human being. Each one of us is far more compulsive, anxious, sexual, high-minded, mean, generous, playful, thoughtful, dazed and at sea than we are ever encouraged to admit.

Part of the reason for our misunderstanding of our normality comes down to a basic fact about our minds: we know through immediate experience what is going on inside us, but only know about other people from what they choose to tell us, which will almost always be a very edited version of the truth.

We know what we've done at 3am, but imagine others sleeping peacefully. We know our somewhat shocking desires from close up; we are left to guess about other people's from what their faces tell us, which is not very much.

This asymmetry between self-knowledge and knowledge-of-others is what lies behind loneliness. We simply can't trust that our deep selves can have counterparts in those we meet, so we stay silent and isolated. The asymmetry encourages shyness too, for we struggle to believe that the imposing, competent strangers we encounter can have any of the vulnerabilities and idiocies we're so familiar with inside our own characters.

Ideally, the task of culture should be to compensate for the failings of our brains by assisting us to a more correct vision of what other people are normally like, by taking us, in a realistic but seductive way, into the inner lives of strangers. This is what novels, films and songs should constantly be doing: defining and evoking states of mind we thought we were alone in experiencing, in order to alleviate our shyness and loneliness.

We are particularly bad at recognising how normal it is to suffer and to be unhappy. Around relationships, for example, we constantly operate with an image of the bliss of others, which mocks and undermines our own efforts to keep going with many flawed but eminently 'good enough' unions. We find it hard to bear in mind that more or less everyone is, beneath a cheery surface, intermittently profoundly sad and rarely not anxious.

We become embarrassed too by our close-up knowledge of our own sexuality, which appears more perverse than that of anyone we know. It almost certainly isn't. We simply haven't been told the full story.

Ideally, art works would offer us a hugely consoling truth: that our hidden worries, the nagging anxieties we keep close to our chests and our stranger thoughts and impulses don't actually make us strange; on the contrary, they are precisely what make us normal. One great goal of the love novel, for instance, should be to tell us what love and long-term relationships are really like so that our own tribulations do not appear so readily as signs that everything is going wrong, but rather that our sufferings are proof that we are in line with common human experience.

Our culture often tries to project an idea of an organised, poised and polished self, as the standard way most people are. We should discount any such myth. Other people are always far more likely to be as we know we are, with all our quirks, fragilities, compulsions and surprising aspects, than they are to be like the apparently 'normal' types we meet in social life.

See also: Anxiety; Art, The Purpose of; Clumsiness; Confidence; Glamour; Good Enough; Inner Idiot, The; Jolliness; Loneliness; Lottery of Life; Politeness; Psychological Asymmetry; Sane Insanity; Sex and Love; Shyness; Ugliness; Vulnerability; Warmth.

O

¶ Oral Sex

Understanding the pleasure of oral sex is central to grasping why sex as a whole might be enjoyable – and why it sometimes inspires us to do what may, on the surface, be some fairly implausible things.

Sucking on another person's genitalia is not, at a physical level, necessarily satisfying in and of itself. The reason why it tends to be experienced as so pleasurable is to be found at the psychological level: it can be ecstatic because it is bound up with the idea of extreme acceptance. Genitals are normally the most private part of ourselves, which we are careful to shield from others, for fear of being judged or of offending. Our mouths, by contrast, are highly visible and respectable elements, the gateway to language and of the expression of rational thought. For someone to allow our mouths to roam freely around their genitals is a supreme sign of having been given unusual access to their deeper selves. It is evidence of being intensely trusted and liked.

A lot about our erotic excitement is bound up with a longing for closeness. Even when we do 'dirty' things (anal play, watersports, BDSM, etc.), the satisfaction is at heart to do with finding someone who is willing to lower their defences and let us into the most guarded spaces of their being.

We are constantly drawn to the idea that sex is primarily about the body but, at its core, sex is a psychological phenomenon. It is the delighted meeting of two previously isolated minds, enacted with the help of limbs and organs performing calculatedly rule-breaking manoeuvres.

Oral sex is exciting first and foremost as a promise of an end to loneliness.

See also: Loneliness.

¶ Original Sin

In the late 4th century, as the immense Roman Empire was collapsing, the leading philosopher of the age, St. Augustine, became deeply interested in possible explanations for the evident tragic disorder of the human world. One central idea he developed was what he legendarily termed *Peccatum Originale:* original sin. Augustine proposed that human nature is inherently damaged and tainted because, in the Garden of Eden, Eve, the mother of all people, sinned against God by eating an apple from the Tree of Knowledge. Her guilt was then passed down to her descendants and now all earthly human endeavours are bound to fail because they are the work of a corrupt and faulty human spirit. This odd idea might not be literally true, of course. However, as a metaphor for why the world is in a mess, it has a beguiling poetic truth, as relevant to atheists as believers. We should perhaps not expect too much from the human race, Augustine implies. We have been somewhat doomed from the outset. And that can, in certain moods, be a highly redemptive thought to keep in mind.

See also: Tragedy.

¶ Other-as-Child

Small children sometimes behave in stunningly unfair and shocking ways: they scream at the person who is looking after them, angrily push away a bowl of animal pasta, throw away something you have just fetched for them. But we rarely feel personally agitated or wounded by their behaviour, because we don't assign a negative motive or mean intention to a small person. We reach for the most benevolent interpretations. We don't think they are doing it in order to upset us. We probably think that they are a bit tired, or that their gums are sore or they are upset by the arrival of a younger sibling. We have a large repertoire of alternative explanations ready in our heads, and none of these lead us to panic or become terribly agitated.

This is the reverse of what tends to happen around adults in general, and our lovers in particular. Here we imagine that others deliberately have us in their sights. If our partner is late for our mother's birthday because of 'work', we may assume it's an excuse. If they promised to buy us some extra toothpaste but then 'forgot', we'll imagine a deliberate slight. They probably relish the thought of causing us a little distress.

But if we employed the infant model of interpretation, our first assumption would be quite different: maybe they didn't sleep well last night and are too exhausted to think straight; maybe they have a sore knee; maybe they are doing the equivalent of testing the boundaries of parental tolerance. Seen from such a point of view, adult behaviour doesn't magically become nice or acceptable. But the level of agitation is kept safely low. It is very touching that we live in a world where we have learnt to be so kind to children; it would be even nicer if we learnt to be a little more generous towards the childlike parts of one another.

Adulthood simply isn't a complete state; what we call childhood lasts (in a submerged but significant way) all our lives. Therefore, some of the moves we execute with relative ease around children must forever continue to be relevant when we're dealing with another grown-up.

The accurate, corrective reimagining of the inner lives of others is a piece of empathetic reflection we constantly need to perform with those around us. We need to imagine the turmoil, disappointment, worry and sheer confusion in people who may outwardly appear merely aggressive or mean.

We do our fellow adults the greatest possible favour when we are able to regard at least some of their bad behaviour as we would those of an infant. We are so alive to the idea that it's patronising to be thought of as younger than we are that we forget that it is also, at times, the greatest privilege for someone to look beyond our adult self in order to engage with – and forgive – the disappointed, furious, inarticulate or wounded child within.

See also: Androcles and the Lion; Charity of Interpretation; Inner Idiot, The; Loving and Being Loved; Universal Love.

¶ Overeating

It is clear that many of us eat too much. In response, a huge industry has grown up that advises us to consume more quinoa, pomegranate and fennel salad and, as often as we can, kale and apple soup. But this is to misunderstand why we start eating excessive amounts. It has nothing to do with food, and therefore trying to change our diet isn't the most logical place to focus our efforts. We eat too much because what we're really hungry for isn't available.

When reaching for a tube of potato chips or biting into yet another burrito, the problem isn't our unconstrained appetite; rather, it is the difficulty we have in getting access to the emotional and psychological nutrients that would feed our broken souls – nutrients that include understanding, tenderness, forgiveness, reconciliation and closeness. We eat too much not because we are (as we brutally accuse ourselves) greedy, but because we live in a world where the emotional ingredients we crave are so elusive.

A vast quantity of human ingenuity has been devoted to enticing the palate, and we have succeeded beyond our wildest expectations. But in the emotional arena, we have hardly begun to supply ourselves reliably with what we long to consume. If we could have ready access to sympathetic friendliness, warmer and calmer relationships with those we love, clearer knowledge of our true ambitions and better self-knowledge around our own failings, our waistlines would be under a lot less pressure.

We continue to eat, not because we are hungry, but because we cannot find anything more satisfying to absorb.

See also: Addiction; Emotional Capitalism.

P

¶ Perfectionism

Perfectionism is the unreasonable and self-defeating ambition of getting something absolutely right, which makes us difficult to be around and punishing to live within.

The origins of perfectionism lie in the imagination, in the ease with which we can conjure up a picture of an ideal state of affairs, compared with the monstrous difficulty of bringing such a state into being by ourselves. The sickness of perfectionism gestates in the fertile gap between our noble visions and our mediocre reality.

Yet our problems do not ultimately arise in our love of perfection per se. They lie in our reckless tendencies to under-budget for the difficulties of achieving it. The proper target for (gentle) criticism is premature perfectionism.

How accurately we budget for time and effort depends on a proper grasp of the inherent difficulty of any task. If we recognise something to be exceptionally arduous, we don't panic when our first efforts are weak and progress slow. It is difficult – but we knew it would be. High standards only become a problem when we think something might and should be substantially easier than it turns out to be, and when we read our struggles as marks of our own ineptitude rather than as an inevitable part of a legitimately lengthy journey.

Perfectionism is only a problem because we have under-budgeted for difficulty, not because we are aiming high. It strikes when we imagine we might write a good novel in six months, or have a good career by the age of thirty, or have spontaneously worked out how to have a successful marriage.

Our perfectionism starts to torture us when we lack information on how hard others had to work and how much they had to suffer before reaching their ideas of perfection. In the Utopia, our culture would endlessly draw to our attention the first drafts and hidden labours of others, and alert us to the true horrors exacted by anything worth doing. We would not then be impatient, sickly perfectionists; we would be patient, resilient questers for excellence.

The problem is not that we're aiming for perfection; it's that we don't have an accurately redemptive idea of what perfection really demands.

See also: Confidence; Expectations; Good Enough; Pessimism.

¶ Pessimism

A pessimist is someone who calmly assumes from the outset, and with a great deal of justification, that things tend to turn out badly in almost all areas of existence. Strange though it can sound, pessimism is one of the greatest sources of human serenity and contentment.

The reasons are legion. Relationships are rarely if ever the blissful marriage of two minds and hearts that Romanticism teaches us to expect; sex is invariably an area of tension and longing; creative endeavour is pretty much always painful, compromised and slow; any job – however appealing on paper – will be irksome in many of its details; children will always resent their parents, however well-intentioned and kindly the adults may try to be. Politics is evidently a process of muddle and unsatisfactory compromise.

Our satisfaction in this life is critically dependent on our expectations. The greater our hopes, the greater the risks of rage, bitterness, disappointment and a sense of persecution.

Many forces in our society conspire to stoke our hopes unfairly. Our commercial and political culture is tragically built upon the manufacture of promises of improbably beautiful scenarios. These forces tap into a natural, though profoundly mistaken, tendency of the human mind to think that the possession of hope must be the key to happiness (and kindness).

Like optimists, pessimists would like things to go well. But by recognising that many things can, and probably will, go wrong, the pessimist is adroitly placed to secure the good outcome both of these parties ultimately seek. It is the pessimist who, having never expected anything to go right, tends to end up with one or two things to smile about.

See also: Anger; Anxiety; Cheerful Despair; Eudaimonia; Existential Angst; Perfectionism; Premeditation; Resilience; Sentimentality.

P

¶ Philosophical Meditation

Our minds are filled with out-of-focus feelings and ideas. We dimly experience a host of regrets, envious feelings, hurts, anxieties and resentments. But for the most part, we never stop to analyse or make sense of these. It seems too painful and difficult, because there is always an extra degree of anxiety that attends the process of beginning to think – whatever the eventual benefits.

However, the weight of our unthought thoughts and unfelt feelings can grow unbearable over time. They take their revenge on us for not giving them the attention they deserve. They wake us up in the middle of the night demanding to be heard; they give us twitches and, one day perhaps, serious illnesses. These neglected feelings and thoughts deserve to be examined and unfurled, for they contain a host of clues as to our future direction and needs. They are not merely clutter, as they might seem under a Buddhist lens; they are the jumbled jigsaw pieces of a future, better self.

It is in order to get a handle on the contents of our minds that we require the practice of Philosophical Meditation. Philosophical Meditation proposes that we regularly set aside a portion of time and systematically set ourselves to answer in detail three core questions: What am I currently anxious about that I haven't properly acknowledged? What am I upset or hurt about that I haven't yet fully understood? And what am I currently excited about that I haven't yet clearly identified or had the courage to integrate into my ambitions?

The practice is built on the notion that our brains won't manage to understand their own content without a considerable degree of artifice and training. We need to establish habits that can regularly prompt us to undertake the arduous work of figuring out what is going on in our own minds.

See also: Addiction; Emotional Intelligence; Emotional Scepticism; Insomnia; News from Within

¶ Philosophy

The best way to understand the true purpose of philosophy is to study its etymology. In Ancient Greek, *philo* means love; *sophia* means wisdom. Philosophy is the grand name given to the quest to lead a wiser life.

At the start of the history of philosophy, Socrates arrived at a novel approach to wisdom. He believed that a huge amount of suffering unfolds because of our inability to use our minds correctly. We don't analyse our emotions; we can't understand our past; we respond with undue haste to certain of our feelings. We haven't begun to understand ourselves.

To this end, he pioneered the basic tools of philosophy: self-analysis, logical examination, introspection, conversation and friendship.

Socrates was the opposite of a disengaged academic: he believed that the only point of thinking was if it could be therapeutic, if it could help us to be slightly less agitated, confused and sorrowful individuals.

The aim of philosophy was – and still is – to help us cope better with our problems by introducing us to accurate and powerful ideas. Philosophy, as Socrates saw it, could be a School of Life.

This dictionary is philosophical in a precisely Socratic sense: it is a list of ideas strictly selected with regard to their usefulness in our lives.

See also: Art for Art's Sake; Culture Can Replace Scripture; Self-Help Books; Wisdom.

P

¶ Politeness

Politeness can sound very boring, a trivial social convention connected up with hypocrisy and perhaps snobbery. Under its dictates, we are urged to say that we've had a nice evening when we haven't really or to tell someone we're delighted by news of their success, when in truth we'd like them dead. Shouldn't we just be frank?

There are some deeply serious reasons why politeness matters. Proceeding politely through the world is founded on a recognition of how easy it is to get things wrong and therefore how important it is not to be quick to anger, not to burn bridges and not to make statements it will be hard to row back from. The polite recognise that their minds have great capacities for error and are subject to moods that will mislead them – and so are keen not to make statements that can't be taken back or to make enemies of people they might decide are in fact worthy of respect down the line.

Sceptical about themselves, polite people will suggest that an idea might be not quite right. They will say that a project is attractive but that it could be interesting to look at alternatives as well. They will consider that an intellectual opponent may well have a point. They aren't just lying or dodging tough decisions. Their behaviour is symptomatic of a nuanced and intelligent belief that few ideas are totally without merit, no proposals are one hundred per cent wrong and almost no one is entirely foolish. They work with a conception of the world in which good and bad are deviously entangled and in which bits of the truth are always showing up in unfamiliar guises in unexpected people. Their politeness is a logical, careful response to the complexity they identify in themselves and in the world.

The polite person also starts with a sense of the vulnerability of others. They know that many they encounter will be only millimetres away from inner collapse, despair and self-hatred. Every piece of neglect, every silence or slightly harsh or off-the-cuff word can have a profound capacity to hurt. So the polite person will be drawn to spend a lot of time noticing and commenting positively on apparently minor facets of others' achievements: they will say that the watercress soup was the best they've had for years and that they'd forgotten how much they liked it; they'll mention that the ending of the writer's new novel made them cry, and that work on the Mexico deal was particularly helpful to, and noticed by, the whole company.

Politeness is not an unnecessary cloak thrown over our innocent natural selves or a minor detail for a metropolitan dinner party: it is the bedrock of civilisation.

See also: Emotional Scepticism; Normality; Secrets in Love; Vulnerability.

¶ Polyamory

Polyamory is the belief in the possibility and nobility of loving (and sleeping with) more than one person at a time, in a situation of mutual consent.

Polyamory can appear a highly mature and workable solution to the tensions between love and sex. It promises that one may not have to choose between a satisfying sex life on the one hand, and a satisfying love life on the other. The two may be combined, by sleeping with and loving a succession of different people. Furthermore, there need be no reason for secrets. Everything one wants can be shared and combined.

Sadly, this promising philosophy has a tendency to forget certain deeply embedded and unfortunate facts about human nature. It overlooks how nice it is when something is fully ours and how worrying it can be when we can no longer make a powerful claim on a person we have learnt to trust. It ignores the pain of not being the centre of another's emotional life. It makes light of jealousy and turns possessiveness into a pathology, rather than an awful but stubborn fact.

The problem with polyamory is not the future it beckons us to. It is what it forgets, along the way, about human beings.

See also: Secrets in Love; Sex and Love.

¶ Pop Music

The ultimate goal of philosophy is to become more like pop music. When pop music started in a big way in the 1960s, it seemed like an especially silly medium, favoured by hormonal schoolgirls and connected with delinquent and bizarre behaviour.

By contrast, philosophy had a reputation for being deeply serious and impressive – the natural home of the big ambition to understand ourselves and transform the world through ideas. But since the 1960s, philosophy has stalled and pop music has conquered the world. It is now the foremost medium for the articulation of ideas on a mass scale. This explains why, if it is to survive, philosophy must study pop; part of its salvation lies in understanding pop's techniques so as to be able to become, in crucial ways, a little more like it.

There are a host of critical lessons philosophy can learn from pop. For a start, pop teaches us about charm. The great pop songs are bewitchingly, dazzlingly charming in the manner in which they get their messages across; they know exactly how to wear away our defences and enter our imaginations with easy grace. It is a reminder that it isn't enough for ideas to be correct. For them to become powerful and deliver on their promises, they need to know how to win over an audience.

Pop is the most seductive force the world has ever known; it has more – and more devoted – adherents than all religions put together. It is more deeply loved, more trusted, and a more constant companion in our joys and sorrows than any other art form.

Pop has become powerful in part because it has cleverly understood the division of labour. Those who can sing and hold the crowd may not be the same as those who know how to write music or arrange instruments. Pop is unashamed about uniting talent wherever it finds it, so the final result can combine the most beautiful face with the finest voice, the best score and the most beguiling instrumental arrangement. Pop has overcome the Romantic hang-up about the unique creator; it knows that the most intimate, heartfelt result may be the outcome of large-scale institutional collaboration.

Pop teaches us too about compression. It knows our lives are busy and has an extraordinarily ambitious sense of what could be achieved in under three minutes. Like all other art forms, pop is trying to communicate ideas, but it bypasses the more resistant intellectual parts of the mind. All the usual obstacles to reaching another person are stripped away in the name of visceral intimacy. Pop achieves what Pericles, Lincoln, Dickens and Proust were attempting – and spectacularly surpasses them all. It provides the ultimate demonstration of the 19th-century theorist Walter Pater's tantalising assertion that 'All art aspires to the condition of music'.

Like religion, pop knows that repetition is key. It works its effect through being heard again and again. It would prefer to grab three minutes from you every day than three hours every two months. Like religious incantation, it is interested in working upon our souls cumulatively. Pop is intelligent enough not to be afraid of simplicity; it is also too wise to be held back by pedantry or erudition. It knows that our emotional needs are in essence obvious: to be encouraged, to be held, to be jollied, to be reassured when we are alone, to be told something beautiful and uplifting. It doesn't suffer from high art's perverse addiction to subtlety. It accepts that the core of our minds may be astonishingly basic in its structure.

Pop is ultimately the master of collective euphoria. It possesses what churches and politicians would like, but are so rarely able, to secure. It has worked out how to generate shared moments of deep emotion about important things. In the stadium, the singer functions as a high priest, for whom the flock might be ready to make major sacrifices; they would, in their benign frenzy, be willing to go anywhere.

That philosophy needs to learn from pop doesn't preclude that pop needs – of course – to learn quite a bit from

P

philosophy as well. Pop currently touches on the big themes but doesn't, as yet, properly take up many of the opportunities that lie in its way. It is lacking in ultimate ambitions. In the future, we need pop musicians to take up the challenge of investigating the deepest truths, of getting behind transformative concepts and of making these into the things we'll sing about in front of the bathroom mirror with our hairbrushes so that they become the background sounds of our inner lives. The world waits for a redemptive synthesis between philosophy and pop.

See also: Akrasia; Cultural Mining; Popularisation; Seduction.

¶ Popularisation

Popularisation has acquired a very bad reputation in certain quarters. To describe someone as a 'good populariser' is to crush them with faint praise. A Romantic prejudice suggests that the mark of true genius is to be of deep interest only to a very few.

Yet the destiny of every properly good idea is to be popular, so the task of good thinking must include not just the formulation of good ideas, but also their powerful and seductive dissemination through society.

The noble populariser realises that sounding dense, hard to understand and elusive is almost always a sign of not having thought hard enough rather than of being a genius. The goal of the populariser is that their ideas should, after a time, start to sound like common sense. The populariser assumes it to be a more complex undertaking to make something sound obvious than to insist on its strangeness. They are more interested in the good of their audience than in their own reputations.

For democracies to succeed, they cannot afford to let good ideas be merely the preserve of the few. They need to democratise not just soap powder and airline travel, but widespread and constant access to the best thoughts and positions – so that tyranny and error can be kept at bay. Collective wisdom depends on the art of popularisation.

See also: Cultural Mining; Culture Can Replace Scripture; Pop Music; Popularity; Seduction.

¶ Popularity

Intellectuals have often been very troubled by the idea of popularity; it seems a deeply wrong guide to what is good, important and serious. They look at some of the most conspicuously popular things (certain newspapers or television shows, for example) and see how shallow and misleading they are. From these examples, it's tempting to draw the conclusion that popularity in itself must be a wicked element.

Yet in a democracy, it's hugely important what happens to be popular. However beautiful and true an idea may be, if it isn't popular, it won't be of any consequence. Instead of condemning popularity, serious people should seek it.

The most successful items of popular culture make certain distinctive moves. They contain clues about how things and ideas get to be popular: they are funny; they intensify drama; they move fast; they are carnal; they never condemn their audiences; they speak from the heart; they are strongly emotional; they acknowledge our fantasies and our darker thoughts; they are direct; they are immensely charming. They are hugely aware of how easily attention is lost, so they seek to entice at every moment.

The currently unpopular, intellectual culture that is ambitious around serious issues faces two choices. Either it can continue to be unpopular, and therefore have very limited consequence in the world, or it can seek to learn the lessons of popularity. It can attempt to make its way into the inner lives of the widest, largest section of the population.

P

Tragically, our sophisticated culture has, in the main, repudiated all the moves that are essential to popularity. But the moves themselves do not corrupt. A truth doesn't become a falsehood for being presented in a sexier or more amusing way. The idea and the vehicle are distinct. Wisdom doesn't become stupidity because a lot of people embrace it. Rather than condemn popular culture, the high-minded should deftly attempt to steal its box of tricks.

See also: Cultural Mining; Culture Can Replace Scripture; Popularisation; Seduction; School of Life, The.

¶ Premeditation

A premeditation is a technical term, invented by the Stoic philosophers of Ancient Greece and Rome, to describe a process, normally to be performed once a day in bed before getting up, whereby one looks into one's future and systematically imagines everything going wrong in it. It is a deliberate, artful, ritualised meditation on varied options for upcoming disasters.

The practice is based on the view that our minds are congenitally unable to face up to the risks we face and do us an enormous disservice through their sentimental, unexamined optimism, leaving us unprepared for the catastrophes that will inevitably come our way. A premeditation constitutes a deliberate attempt to bring our expectations into line with the troubles we face. It builds on a fundamental idea about anger: that we don't get angry simply because something bad has happened; we grow furious only when it is bad and unexpected.

The Stoic philosopher Seneca believed that the greatest service we can pay ourselves is to crush hope. Here is an example of a Senecan premeditation:

The wise will start each day with the thought: fortune gives us nothing which we can really own. Whatever has been built up over years is scattered and dispersed in a single day. No, he who has said "a day" has granted too long; an hour, an instant, suffices for the overthrow of empires. Look at your wrists, a falling tile could cut them. Look at your feet, a paving stone could render you unable to walk again. We live in the middle of things that have all been destined to be damaged and to die. Mortal have you been born, to mortals have you given birth. Reckon on everything, expect everything.

Of course, premeditation doesn't remove the bad things. But by getting us to admit, frankly and bravely, that we are likely to encounter hell one day, it can leave us a little less distraught when it eventually comes our way.

Ideally, our culture would do some of the work of premeditation for us: it would constantly feed us – through a wise emotional education delivered via culture – certain realistic ideas about the sadly demanding and radically imperfect nature of existence. But until it can overcome its congenital sentimentality, we should take care never to start the day without our own private premeditation.

See also: Anger; Pessimism; Resilience; Sentimentality.

¶ Procrastination

Procrastination is often mistaken for laziness, but is really a species of terror at the possible consequences of messing up. The best way to address the disease is to reduce the imaginative spectre of failure and gently raise the spectre of inaction, which is never cost-free. We get down to work when the fear of doing nothing at all finally exceeds the fear of doing it badly.

See also: Good Enough; Teaching and Learning.

¶ Psychological Asymmetry

One of the most basic facts about the human condition is that we know ourselves from the inside, but know others only from what they choose or are able to tell us – a far more limited and edited set of data.

We are continuously and intimately exposed to our own worries, hopes, desires and memories, many of which feel overwhelmingly intense, strange, vulnerable or sad. Yet when it comes to others, we are restricted to knowing them through their public pronouncements, to what they can or choose to reveal. The hints and clues we are left to play with are hugely imperfect guides to the reality of another person's existence.

The result of this Psychological Asymmetry is that we almost always think of ourselves as far more peculiar, shameful and alarming than other people. Our experiences of anxiety, anger, envy, sex and distress appear to be so much more intense and disturbing than those of anyone in the vicinity. In truth, of course, we aren't really so odd; we just know a lot more about who we are.

The results of Psychological Asymmetry are loneliness and shyness. We are beset by loneliness because we cannot imagine that others long and desire, envy and hate, crave and weep as we do. We feel ourselves cast out into a world of strangers, inherently different from everyone we live alongside, and potentially offensive to all those who might know us properly. In dark moments, it appears that no one could possibly both know and like us.

We also become shy and are easily intimidated by people who we assume cannot share in our vulnerabilities and who we imagine would be entirely unable to relate to the petty, grand, perverse or idealistic thoughts that pass moment by moment through our minds. If we reach important positions, we feel like impostors, beset by an impression that our quirks separate us from others who have occupied comparable roles in the past. We grow boring and conventional, mimicking the externals of other people on the false assumption that this is what they might truly be like inside.

The solutions to Psychological Asymmetry lie in two places: art and love. Art provides us with accurate portrayals of the inner lives of strangers and, with grace and compelling charm, shows us how much they share in troubles and hopes we thought we might be alone in experiencing. And love gives us an occasional, deeply precious, sense of security to reveal who we really are to another person and the opportunity to learn about their reality from a position of secure proximity.

To overcome the effects of Psychological Asymmetry, we must trust that most people are far closer to what we are (that is, far shyer, more scared, more worried and more incomplete) than they are to resembling the personas they show to the world. Fortunately, none of us is quite as odd, or quite as special, as we might assume or fear.

P

See also: Impostor Syndrome; Loneliness; Normality; Shyness; Vulnerability.

Q

¶ Quiet Life, The

A quiet life sounds like an option that only the defeated would ever be inclined to praise. The age is overwhelmingly alive to the benefits of active, social, complex and ambitious ways of living. Lauding a quiet life has some of the eccentricity of praising rain.

We are suspicious because the defenders of quiet lives have so often come from the most implausible sections of the community – slackers, hippies, the work-shy, the fired – those who seem like they never had a choice; people whose quiet lives appear to have been imposed upon them by their own ineptitude.

Yet, when we examine things further, busy lives turn out to have so many incidental costs that we have been collectively committed to ignoring. At the top, alongside our privileges, we may grow impoverished in curious ways. We may be able to shut down a factory in India, and our every word may be listened to with trembling respect within a vast organisation, but what we cannot do is admit that we are extremely tired and want to spend the afternoon reading on the sofa. We grow strangers to those who love us outside of our wealth and status, while depending ever more on the fickle attention of those for whom we are our achievements alone. Our children see ever less of us. Our spouses grow bitter. We may own the wealth of continents, but it has been ten years at least since we last had the chance to do nothing for a day.

At this point in history, we are so fixated on the idea that poverty must always be involuntary and therefore the result of lack of talent and indigence, we have trouble imagining that it might be the result of an intelligent and skilled person's free choice based on a rational evaluation of costs and benefits. It might sincerely be possible for someone to decide not to take the better-paid job, not because they had no chance, but because – having surveyed the externalities involved – they did not think them worth it.

When we come to know the true price some ways of life exact, we may realise we are not willing to pay for the envy, fear, deceit and anxiety. Our days on earth are limited. For the sake of true riches, we may willingly, and with no loss of dignity, opt to become a little more reclusive, temperate and obscure.

See also: Bounded Work; Domesticity; Flowers; Small Pleasures.

Q

R

¶ Resilience

One of the characteristic flaws of our minds is to exaggerate how fragile we might be; to assume that life would be impossible far earlier than in fact it would be.

We imagine that we could not live without a certain kind of income, status or health; that it would be a disaster not to have a certain kind of relationship, house or job. This natural tendency of the mind is constantly stoked by life in commercial society. This kind of society goes to extraordinary lengths to make us feel that we really need to go skiing once a year, to have heated car seats, to fly in business class, to own the same kind of watch as a famous conductor, and to lay claim to lots of friends, perfectly muscular health and a loving, kind, sex-filled relationship.

In fact, our core needs are much simpler than this. We could manage perfectly well with very much less – not just around possessions, but across every aspect of our lives. It's not that we should want to, it's simply that we could. We could cope quite well with being rather poor, not being very popular, not having a very long life and with living alone. To put the extreme instance forwards, we could even cope with being dead; it happens all the time.

But we forget our resilience in the face of the risks we face. The cumulative effect of our innocence is to make us timid. Our lives become dominated by a fear of losing, or never getting, things that we could do perfectly well without.

The Ancient Roman philosopher Seneca had great success running what we would now call a venture capital firm.

He owned beautiful villas and magnificent furniture. But he made a habit of regularly sleeping on the floor of an outhouse and eating only stale bread and drinking lukewarm water. He was reminding himself that it wouldn't be so bad to lose nearly everything, so as to free himself from nagging worries of catastrophe. The realisation gave him great confidence. He never worried so much about what might happen if a deal went wrong because, at the very worst, he'd only be back on the kitchen floor next to the dog basket – which was OK in the scheme of things.

Seneca was initiating an important move. By continually renewing our acquaintance with our own resilience – that is, with our ability to manage even if things go badly (getting sacked, a partner walking out, a scandal that destroys our social life, an illness) – we can be braver, because we grasp that the dangers we face are almost never as great as what our skittish imaginations tend to suggest.

In the Utopia, our culture would stop continually presenting us with rags to riches stories. It would instead do something far kinder and more conducive to the kind of courageous, entrepreneurial optimism our societies currently ineptly try to foster.

Our culture would be continually presenting us with charming non-tragic tales of riches to rags stories, tales in which people lost money, partners and social standing but ended up coping rather well with their new lives. We'd see them moving out of the penthouse into a humble cottage and having a fairly nice time tending to a small flowerbed and discovering tinned food. Our culture would not be recommending such scenarios, just lessening the grip upon us of certain deep but misplaced fears that so often hold us back from trying and succeeding.

See also: Anger; Cheerful Despair; Eudaimonia; Existential Angst; Faulty Walnut, The; Pessimism; Premeditation; Sentimentality; Ugliness.

¶ Ritual

Modern culture is very attached to the idea of doing things only once and then moving on to fresh experiences. Novelty and change are centrally prestigious notions; we're eager to explore new places, ideas and opportunities. This attitude comes into particular focus around the status we accord to 'the news', a medium that fundamentally equates novelty with importance.

Correspondingly, we assume there could be nothing more ridiculous than repeating an old idea again and again. Repetition sounds boring and irksome, like the worst experiences of childhood education. But other cultures have taken a different and perhaps wiser view; they have had a high regard for repetition. They have created aesthetically compelling occasions where the same lesson has been rehearsed again and again. Across the globe and through time, it is particularly religions that have been concerned with getting people to repeat ideas. Zen Buddhists have looked at the moon every autumn and written poems in its honour on a set day; Jews will take time to appreciate spring according to a ritual requirement of their holy calendar; Catholics are required to ritually examine their consciences every Sunday; in Russia, Orthodox ritual demanded that before a long journey, everyone would meditate briefly on the possibility of never seeing each other again.

What fired the religious devotion to ritual was the realisation that if the goal was to change minds and behaviour (and thereby change the world), once was never going to be enough.

In a secular age, the deep link between religion and ritual has served to cast the very concept of repetition into shadow. This is unfair. In the Utopia, the most important ideas would keep being reinforced via aesthetically compelling rituals. On a regular basis, we would be reminded of the importance of forgiveness, appreciation, self-knowledge and kindness. It's not that we ever actively disagree with such ideas; we simply forget to act upon them in practice. We need rituals to ensure that we properly listen to the significance of all the old things we half-know already, but avoid properly putting into practice nevertheless.

See also: Akrasia; Memento Mori; Saints; Secularisation.

¶ Rock Appreciation

It might strike us as odd to put a smallish rock in a place of honour on a pedestal. It's not that we hate rocks; it's just that we don't normally find them very interesting. But in China things have been very different: for centuries, poets and artists have been obsessed with the varied charms of irregularly shaped and strikingly coloured lumps of stone.

The poet Mi Fu liked to pay compliments to a dramatically weathered rock and wrote tenderly about its resilience and dignity. The most favoured rocks were dark and glossy, quarried from the limestone of Lingbi, in the northern Anhui province. The best examples might cost as much as a house.

Under the influence of this tradition, we might start to pay a lot more admiring attention to the rocks we ourselves happen to come across. But we'd have to go to China for this inspiration, because our culture doesn't offer us many prompts of encouragement in this rock direction. Our culture has, however, taken great pains to get us to see what might be nice about other things: the pleasures of fine dining, attending the Olympic opening ceremony or flying business class. But when we encounter the tradition of rock homage in China, we are alerted to how many other things still remain to be appreciated in a host of areas of life, if only we were invited to turn our gaze towards them and given a few guiding hints about what to look for.

Our lives are, in part, a search for pleasure. The irony is that we may, via a limited culture, be missing many sources

R

Guo Xu, *Mi Fu Honouring a Rock*, 1503.
The poet Mi Fu was one of many Chinese appreciators of the beauty of weathered rock.

The fact that the special qualities of rocks are often overlooked in Western culture
indicates just how many things in life could benefit from our attention and appreciation.

of great enjoyment that are readily available and within our reach –including the occasional lump of limestone or granite.

See also: Appreciation; Art, The Purpose of; Small Pleasures; Water Towers.

¶ Romantic

Romanticism is a movement of art and ideas that began in Europe in the mid-18th century and has now taken over the world. It is hard to go far on almost any issue without encountering a dominant Romantic position.

At the core of the Romantic attitude is a trust in feeling and instinct as supreme guides to life, and a corresponding suspicion of reason and analysis. In relation to love, this inspires a belief that passionate emotions will reliably guide us to a partner who can provide us with fifty years or so of intimate happiness. It also leads to a veneration of sex as the ultimate expression of love (a position that turns adultery from a problem into a disaster). In relation to work, the Romantic spirit leads to a faith in spontaneous 'genius' and a trust that all talented people will experience the pull of a vocation. In social life, Romanticism argues against politeness and convention and in favour of frankness and plain speaking. It assumes that children are pure and good, and that it is only ever society that corrupts them. Romanticism hates institutions and venerates the brave outsider who fights heroically against the status quo. It likes what is new rather than recurring. The Romantic spirit pits itself against analysis; it believes there is such a thing as 'thinking too much' (rather than just thinking badly). It doesn't favour logic or discourse. Music is its favourite artistic medium. It is offended by what is humdrum and ordinary and longs for the special, the rare,

R

Eugène Delacroix, *Liberty Leading the People*, 1830.
An invitation to Romanticism.

the distinctive and the exclusive. It likes revolution rather
than evolution. The Romantic attitude disdains organisation,
punctuality, clarity, bureaucracy, industry, commerce and
routine. It admits that these things are necessary, but considers
them 'un-Romantic': miserable impositions forced upon us
by the unfortunate conditions of existence.

The supreme symbol of the Romantic attitude is Eugène
Delacroix's legendary painting *Liberty Leading the People*.

Romanticism has its distinctive wisdom, but in many areas
its central messages have become a catastrophic liability in
our lives. They push us in decisively unhelpful directions;
they incite unreal hopes, make us impatient with ourselves,
discourage introspection, blind us to the dangers of obeying
instinct in love and work, turn us away from our realities
and lead us to lament the normal conditions of existence.

The huge task of our age is to unwind Romantic attitudes and replace them with an outlook that might, for the sake of symmetry and historical accuracy, be called Classical.

See also: Changing the World; Classical; FOMO; Genius.

¶ Romantic Disappointment

Often our partner isn't terrible in any big way but we feel a growing sadness about our relationship: they're not as focused on us as we'd hoped; they don't understand us fully; they're preoccupied, a bit abrupt, not hugely interested in the details of our day; they call their friends rather than talk with us. We feel disenchanted and let down, and may start to think we're with the wrong person.

This sorrow has a paradoxical source: early childhood. At the best moments of childhood, a loving parent offered us extraordinary satisfaction. They knew when we were hungry or tired, even though we couldn't explain. They made us feel completely safe. They were enchanted by our smallest achievements. We were entertained and indulged.

As adults, we continue to be in thrall to this notion of being loved, and find our partners sorely wanting as a result. It's a natural but profoundly unfair comparison. For a start, our needs were so much simpler. We didn't need someone to trawl intelligently through the troubled corners of our minds and understand why it is necessary to see our aunt on Sunday, why it matters to us that the curtains harmonise with the sofa covers, or why bread must be cut with a proper bread knife. Our partner is stumbling in the dark around needs that are immensely subtle, far from obvious and very complicated to deliver on.

Secondly, in the early days, none of it was reciprocal. The parent was intensely focused on caring for us, but they knew

R

and totally accepted that we wouldn't engage with their needs. They didn't need us to ask them about their day or make sense of their anxieties.

Our parents were probably kind enough to shield us from the burden that looking after us imposed on them: they maintained a reasonably sunny façade until they retired to their own bedroom, at which point the true toll of their efforts could be witnessed (but by then we were asleep).

The source of our present sorrow is not, therefore, that our adult lovers are tragically inept or uniquely selfish. It's rather that we're judging our adult experiences in the light of a very different kind of childhood love. We are sorrowful not because we have landed with the wrong person, but because we have grown up.

See also: Love as Generosity; Loving and Being Loved.

¶ Romantic Instinct

For most of history, relationships were a rational business, to do with matching land, status and religion. Marriages were cold, ruthless and almost wholly disconnected from the happiness of their protagonists.

What replaced the Marriage of Reason was the Marriage of Instinct, an arrangement that dictated that feeling should be the supreme guide to the formation of good relationships. Passionate emotion became viewed as the ideal predictor of fifty years of conjugal happiness.

We have grown used to following our hearts. Unfortunately, only too often, these hearts prove troublingly deceptive and unreliable. Our instincts pull us not so much towards situations that will make us happy as situations that feel familiar, which might be quite a different thing.

This is because adult love intimately rehearses the themes of childhood love, and a great many of us learnt of love in childhood in less than ideal conditions. The love we tasted when we were small will likely have involved not only tenderness and affection but also (in some form or other) troublesome dynamics: there might have been depression, anger, withdrawal, abandonment, favouritism, a pressure to succeed, or a subtle call to fail.

When we reach adulthood, our 'instinct' then has a habit of impelling us towards situations that echo the less than ideal themes of childhood: we seek to find people of similar emotional maturity to our childhood caregivers. This explains why we so often find ourselves rejecting candidates who might on paper be eminently well matched and mature. Yet we cannot muster enthusiasm, and complain that they are 'boring' or 'not sexy'. What we may at a subliminal level mean is: simply not disturbed enough to make us suffer in the ways we need to suffer in order to feel that love is real.

The time has come to outgrow our veneration of 'instinct'. We need relationships in which our feelings have been properly submitted to examination and brought under the aegis of a mature awareness of our long and always distinctively troubled psychological histories.

See also: Crushes; Emotional Scepticism; Faulty Walnut, The; Long-Term Love.

R

S

¶ Saints

The idea of a saint can sound very remote from the normal concerns of modern life. But the religious tradition of saints encapsulates an important idea that isn't necessarily tied to religion at all.

Saints were once identified and venerated by churches in an attempt to promote important ideas via the lives and characters of specific people. A saint might be famous for being very kind (like St. Francis of Assisi) or for staying cheerful in a demanding office job (like St. Philip Neri, whose catchphrase was 'Let me get through today'); or a parent who was extremely patient with a difficult child (like St. Monica). The point about a saint wasn't simply that they were very good or holy, but that they had some specific and very important lesson to teach us.

Nowadays, we still hero-worship, but we focus on people who are unusually talented, powerful or beautiful. They have nothing in particular to impart to us, other than – unwittingly – to humiliate us for being so ordinary. The idea of a saint holds out a more realistic and wiser option: that we should channel admiration for others in directions that will help us manage our own lives better.

The decline in religious belief has not made the underlying thesis behind saints irrelevant. There is an idea within them that needs to be rescued. Human beings need role models. We shouldn't complain about or eradicate role models; we need to improve the genre, bringing a better sort of person to the fore of public consciousness. We need better celebrities rather than no celebrities.

We should take more seriously the task of creating 'good celebrities', versions of secular saints who demonstrate with seductive clarity virtues that need to be more prominent in society. As part of this venture, one might, for example, set up prizes to locate: 'The introvert who most successfully managed to communicate what he/she felt to their partner'; 'The child who most generously forgave their parents'; 'The worker who most intelligently defused infighting at the office', or, the most elusive target of all: 'The husband who best learnt to control his temper and say sorry.'

Being good won't ever be the result merely of hearing lectures on the subject; it requires that we see goodness enacted in the lives of intermittently ordinary but profoundly charming and inspiring people all around us.

See also: Good Nationalism; Nagging; Ritual; Secularisation; Seduction.

¶ Sane Insanity

It does not lie within any of our remits to be entirely sane. There are so many powerful reasons why we must lack an entirely even keel. We have complex histories, we are heading towards the ultimate catastrophe, we are vulnerable to devastating losses; love will never go wholly well, the gap between our hopes and our realities will be cavernous. In the circumstances, what we should aim for is not sanity, but a wise, knowledgeable and self-possessed relationship to our manifold insanities, or what we might term 'Sane Insanity'. The sane insane differ from the simply insane by virtue of the honest and accurate grasp they have on what is not entirely right with them. They may not be wholly balanced, but they don't have the additional folly of insisting on their normalcy. They can admit with good grace, and no particular loss of

S

dignity, that they are rather peculiar in a myriad of ways. They do not go out of their way to hide from us what they get up to in the night, in their sad moments, when anxiety strikes, or during attacks of envy. At their best they can be dryly funny about the tragedy of being human. They lay bare the fears, doubts, longings, desires and habits that don't belong to the story we like to tell ourselves about sanity. They don't make ready confessions to let themselves off the hook or to be eccentric. They simply realise the unreasonableness of expecting to be reasonable all the time. They warn others as far as possible in advance of what being around them might involve, and apologise promptly for their failings as soon as they have manifested themselves. They offer their friends and companions accurate maps to their craziness, which is about the most generous thing one can do to anyone who has to endure us. The sane insane among us are not a special category of the mentally unwell: they represent the most evolved possibility for a mature human being.

See also: Art, The Purpose of; Confidence; Loneliness; Normality; Shyness; Vulnerability.

¶ School of Life, The

The School of Life is an organisation devoted to fostering emotional intelligence, better relationships, more meaningful careers, better architecture, higher levels of wisdom, a nobler kind of capitalism, eudaimonia and cheerful despair.

See also: Popularity; Success at School vs. Success in Life; the rest of this book.

¶ Secrets in Love

Our ideal of Romantic love has at its heart the notion that a truly good relationship is one in which we are able to tell a partner everything.

At last, there will be no more need for the usual hypocrisies. We will be able to come clean about so much that we had previously needed to keep to ourselves: our reservations about our friends; our irritation over small but wounding remarks by colleagues; our interest in rarely mentioned sexual practices. Love seems founded on the idea of radical disclosure.

But gradually, we stand to become aware of so much we cannot say. It might be around sex: on a work trip we flirted with a colleague and nearly let our hand touch theirs; we discovered a porn site that beautifully targeted a special quirk of our erotic imagination; we find our partner's brother or sister very alluring. Or the secret thoughts can be more broad-ranging: the blog they wrote for work, about their experience in client care, was very boring; they are putting on weight around their waist; their best friend from school, to whom they are still loyal, is (in our view) excessively silly and dull; in the wedding photo of their parents (lovingly displayed in a silver frame in the living room) their mother looks very smug.

Love begins with a hope of unburdening ourselves entirely and overcoming loneliness forever. The initial relief of honesty is at the heart of the feeling of being 'in love'. But this sharing of secrets sets up in our minds – and in our collective culture – a hugely problematic ideal: that if two people love one another, they must always tell each other the truth about everything.

The idea of honesty is sublime. It presents a deeply moving vision of how two people can be together, and it is a constant presence in the early months. But in order to be kind, and in order to sustain love, it ultimately becomes necessary to keep many thoughts out of sight.

Keeping secrets can seem like a betrayal of the relationship. At the same time, the complete truth invariably places

S

any union in mortal danger. Much of what we'd ideally like to have recognised and confirmed is going to be genuinely disturbing even to someone who is fond of us.

We face a choice between honesty and acceptability and – for reasons that deserve a great deal of sympathy – mostly we choose the latter. We are perhaps too conscious of the bad reasons for hiding something; we haven't paid enough attention to the noble reasons why, from time to time, true loyalty may lead us to say very much less than the whole truth. We are so impressed by honesty that we have forgotten the virtues of politeness – this word defined not as a cynical withholding of important information for the sake of harm, but as a dedication to not rubbing someone else up against the true, hurtful aspects of our nature. It is ultimately no great sign of kindness to insist on showing someone our entire selves at all times. Repression, a certain degree of restraint and a dedication to editing our pronouncements belong to love as much as a capacity for explicit confession. The person who cannot tolerate secrets, who in the name of 'being honest' divulges information so wounding it cannot be forgotten, is no friend of love. We should accept an ongoing need to edit our full reality.

See also: Infidelity; Politeness; Polyamory; Sex and Love.

¶ Secularisation

Secularisation is the process whereby humanity has gradually divested itself of its long-held beliefs in deities and gods. Almost all of the world's most developed countries have, over the past century, undergone a significant process of secularisation. Religions that were once immensely influential across the whole of society now usually have only tiny bands of faithful adherents.

It might be assumed that secularisation logically involves one thing only: proving the non-existence of a god and then ridding the world of everything related to religion.

But there may be a different way to approach secular-isation – a nuance that relates back to the dual identity of religions. Aside from their grandly speculative notions about the origins of the universe and the survival of the soul after death, religions have also been the carriers of a range of useful and important psychological ideas. Religions have been engaged in two tasks: to make us faithful and to make us wise.

For long periods of history, religions were involved not only in metaphysical speculations, but also in what we would now call emotional education. They foregrounded forgiveness, char-ity, community, ritual gratitude, honesty about one's failings, generosity towards the weak and a rejection of money as the ultimate measure of the worth of individuals.

Religions were also astonishingly inventive about how to bring this emotional education about. They didn't just deliver dry lectures in ugly classrooms. They deployed the greatest artists in the world to make their views of the well-lived life seductively convincing; they built the finest buildings and commissioned the greatest art in an attempt to get difficult messages about kindness, generosity, humility and sorrow to lodge firmly in our souls. They mined the power of ritual: they realised how repetition, rules, special clothes, sacred foods and days, words and gestures might help our leaky brains retain important ideas.

The true task of secularisation is to steal from the educa-tional techniques of religions while disregarding (most of) their content. Religions are intermittently too creative, interesting and useful to be abandoned merely to those who happen to believe in them. The priority is to rescue some of what is still wise, inspiring and relevant from all that is no longer true.

See also: Akrasia; Culture Can Replace Scripture; Day of Judgement; Emotional Capitalism; Emotional Education; Monasteries; Ritual; Saints; Seduction; Self-Help Books.

¶ Seduction

Seduction is the attempt to get any set of tricky ideas into the mind of another person using the arts of charm. Although we know the concept of seduction well enough in romantic contexts, the manoeuvre is of huge relevance far beyond this. Managing employees requires seduction; instilling discipline in children requires seduction; and leading a country involves seduction.

Unfortunately, the idea of 'seduction' has acquired a bad name. If a book is charmingly written, if a song makes people want to dance, if a product is well marketed, if a person has a winning smile and sweet manners, suspicions develop only too easily.

Yet the idea of seduction is vital to any educational mission, for the ideas that we most need to hear are almost always the ones that we would in some ways like to ignore, and therefore need maximal help in absorbing.

We need the toughest lessons to be coated in the most subtle and inventive charm. We need an alliance of education and seduction.

At certain historical moments, the point has been well heeded. The central philosopher of the Renaissance, Marsilio Ficino, wished to teach the population of Florence to live according to the highest principles of virtue and intelligence. But he also knew the human mind well; he understood that it was no use delivering lectures if genuine change on a large scale was required. Therefore, he persuaded his patrons, the wealthy Medici family, to harness the seductive skills of Italy's finest artists to a broad and subtly concealed educational programme.

Magnificent buildings and sensuously appealing works of art were allied to the noblest lessons of Classical and Biblical authors. Madonnas on altarpieces became not only kind and gentle-looking, but also plainly rather sexy, for – as Ficino knew – we have a habit of listening a little more closely when the person speaking to us is someone we might subliminally want to undress.

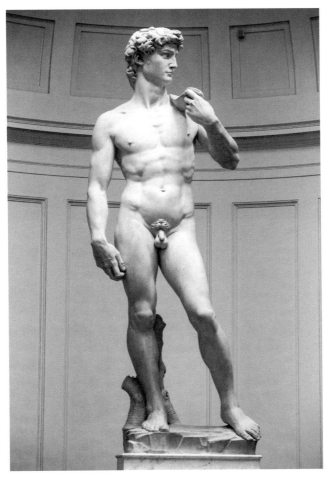

Michelangelo, *David*, 1501–04.
This strikingly handsome nude statue helped to deliver a
key intellectual message about political independence in
Renaissance Florence in a seductive way.

S

Altar in the pilgrimage church of the Fourteen Holy Saints, Wallfahrtskirche
Vierzehnheiligen, Bavaria. Constructed 1743–1772.
The lavishly decorated interior of this church helped seduce people into accepting the
messages preached within it – or so hoped the preachers, anyway.

When Michelangelo (Ficino's pupil) placed his statue *David* in front of the government building in Florence, it was the sexiest, most alluring statue Europe had witnessed since the fall of Rome. David looked irresistible, but he was also the carrier of a key intellectual argument, derived from Cicero, about how the independence of a state must be founded on the capacity for courage and sacrifice.

Similarly, in 18th-century Bavaria, moralist preachers wanted to promote compassion for the suffering of strangers, sorrow for our own selfishness and the spiritual significance of Jesus's view of existence. But they were conscious of how easily we might ignore such ideas in already busy and tricky lives. So, very deliberately, they set out to seduce.

With the help of the finest Baroque architects, they constructed ornate and richly carved churches that provoked admiration, awe and love. It became a little easier to believe in the ideas that had sponsored these masterpieces after a few hours under their magnificent domes.

The urge to nag is very understandable, especially when a lesson is important. But sadly, nagging – the insistent, urgent, graceless repetition of a message – will only ever work for a small number of people who are almost on side anyway. It cannot change humanity.

This sets up a tragic situation: what naggers have to say may be supremely important, but their manner of delivery ensures it will never be heard.

Seduction can always be used in the service of nefarious ends. But in the Utopia, there would be strategic alliances between the deepest, most sincere, thinkers and the most seductive voices and creators. Seductive techniques would be carefully deployed to make sure that what really mattered reliably worked its way into the hearts and minds of pretty much everyone.

See also: Akrasia; Art, The Purpose of; Art and News; Changing the World; Cultural Mining; Glamour; Memento Mori; Nagging; Pop Music; Popularisation; Popularity; Saints; Secularisation; State Broadcasting; Teaching and Learning.

¶ Self-Help Books

There is no more ridiculed literary genre than the self-help book. Intellectually minded people universally scorn the idea of them. Self-help books don't appear on reading lists at any prestigious university; they're not reviewed by highbrow journals, and it's inconceivable that a major literary prize could ever be awarded to one of their authors.

This concerted attack on the entire genre of self-help is a symptom of a Romantic prejudice against the idea of emotional education. Offering explicit emotional education is regarded as beneath the dignity of any serious writer. If we are at all intelligent, we should know how to live already.

S

Unsurprisingly, therefore, the quality of self-help books is at present highly degraded. The most accomplished stylists and sharpest thinkers would feel ashamed to put their name to a work that would be destined to end up on the most mocked shelves of any bookshop.

Yet not all eras have shared this dismissive attitude. In the Classical culture of Ancient Greece and Rome, it was taken for granted that the highest ambition of any author was to offer the reader an emotional education that could guide them towards fulfilment (eudaimonia). Self-help books were at the pinnacle of literature. The most admired thinkers – Plato, Aristotle, Cicero, Seneca, Plutarch and Marcus Aurelius – all wrote self-help books, whose aim was to teach us to live well and die well. Furthermore, they deployed every resource of intelligence, wit and style in writing their manuals to ensure that their messages would delight readers' intellectual as well as emotional faculties. Seneca's *On Anger* and Marcus Aurelius's *Meditations* are among the greatest works of literature of any nation or era. They are also, undeniably, self-help books.

It can look as if humans stopped writing good self-help after the Fall of Rome. But once we view culture as a tool for emotional education, many more works emerge as belonging to the currently much-maligned genre. For example, Tolstoy's *War and Peace* explicitly aims to teach compassion, calm and forgiveness; it offers guidance around money, manners, relationships and career development; it seeks to show us how to be a good friend and how to be a better parent. It clearly is a self-help book – it just isn't officially described this way by the current guardians of culture. Similarly, Marcel Proust's *In Search of Lost Time* is a self-help book, teaching us how to surrender our attachment to romantic love and social status in favour of a focus on art and ideas.

It is not an insult to describe masterpieces as self-help books. It is a way of correctly identifying their ambitions, which are to guide us away from folly towards more sincere and authentic lives. Such works show us that self-help shouldn't be a low-grade marginal undertaking and that the desire to guide and teach wisdom is at the core of all ambitious writing.

In the bookstores of the Utopia, the self-help shelves would be the most prestigious. On them would sit the most distinguished works of world literature – returned, at last, to their true home.

See also: Art for Art's Sake; Culture Can Replace Scripture; Emotional Education; Eudaimonia; Philosophy; Secularisation.

¶ Self-Knowledge

One of the most striking features of our minds is how little we understand them. Although we inhabit ourselves, we seldom manage to make sense of more than a fraction of who we are. It can be easier to master the dynamics of another planet than to grasp what is at play in the folds of our own brains.

Instances of self-ignorance surprise and perturb us at regular intervals: on certain days, we can be irritable or sad without any idea why. Or we may feel lost in our career, but be unable to say more than that we wish to 'do something creative' or 'help make the world a better place' – plans so vague that they leave us perilously vulnerable to the more robust ambitions of others.

It has been the achievement of psychology to instil in us a sense of a basic division between two parts of the mind – the conscious and the unconscious; between what is immediately accessible to us and what lies in shadow, and will surprise us in symptoms, dreams, slips of the tongue and diffuse anxieties, longings and fears. It has also been the work of psychology to insist that maturity must involve a constant drive to turn what is unconscious conscious: to help us master the art of self-knowledge.

S

We need not blame ourselves for our poor grasp of our own minds. The problem is inherent in the very architecture of the brain, an organ that evolved over millennia for the sake of rapid, instinctive decision-making – not the patient, introspective sifting of ideas and emotions.

But a degree of emotional squeamishness is also responsible for our failure to look inside. A lot of what is unconscious is tricky material that we long not to have to look at too closely. For example, we may feel troublingly angry towards people we thought we loved. We may be more ruthless and envious than nice people are ever meant to be. We may have to make enormous changes to our lives, but prefer the ease of the status quo. Across childhood, we may have had instilled in us, so subtly that we didn't even notice, strong notions about what are and are not normal things to experience. We may have picked up covert but forceful indications that no decent person (no one loved by their parents, at least) could be unable to cope at work, tempted by an affair or still upset over a break-up that happened three years ago. Most of our sexual desires still have no place in our standard understanding of respectability.

When difficult feelings do threaten to emerge, the light of consciousness can be counted upon to take fright and shine its beam elsewhere. By failing to investigate the recesses of the mind, we carefully protect our self-image and can continue to think rather well of ourselves. But we don't escape from the job of introspection lightly. There is almost always a high price to pay for our reluctance to look within. Feelings and desires that haven't been examined tend not to leave us alone. They linger and spread their energy randomly to neighbouring issues. Ambition that doesn't know itself comes out as anxiety. Envy comes out as bitterness; anger turns into rage; sadness into depression. Disavowed material buckles and strains the system. We develop pernicious tics: a facial twitch, impotence, an incapacity to work, alcoholism, a porn compulsion. Most so-called 'addictions' are at heart symptoms of insistent difficult feelings that we haven't found a way to address. Insomnia is revenge for thoughts we have refused to have in the day.

Strangers to ourselves, we end up making bad choices: we exit a relationship that might have been at heart quite workable. We don't explore our own professional talents in time. We alienate friends through erratic and off-putting behaviour. We lack insight into how we come across to others and appal or shock. We buy the wrong things and go on holiday to places that have little to do with what we really enjoy. It is no coincidence that Socrates should have boiled down the entire wisdom of philosophy to one simple command: know yourself.

It's a distinctly odd-sounding ambition. Society has no shortage of people and organisations offering to guide us around distant continents, but very few that will help us with the arguably far more important task of travelling around the byways of our minds.

Fortunately, there are a number of tools and practices that can help us to reach inside our minds and move us from dangerous vagueness to challenging but redeeming clarity.

See also: Philosophical Meditation; Unprocessed Emotion.

¶ Self-Sabotage

S

It is normal to expect that we will always actively seek out our own happiness in relationships and careers, yet we often act as if we were deliberately out to ruin our chances. When going on dates, we may lapse into unnecessarily opinionated and antagonistic behaviour. In relationships, we may drive well-intentioned partners to distraction through repeated unwarranted accusations and angry explosions. At work, we may stumble before the biggest chances.

Such behaviour can't always be put down to mere bad luck. It may deserve a stronger, more intentional term: Self-Sabotage. We destroy our opportunities because of a background sense that success is undeserved; this breeds a compulsion to bring our outer reality into line with our inner one, so that we end up being as unsuccessful as we feel.

Hope is hard for self-saboteurs to endure. It may feel internally easier to destroy one's happiness oneself, at a time of one's own choosing, rather than to wait for circumstances to do the trick for one (as they surely will), when one is unprotected and trusting. Failing feels grim but – at least – safely grim.

Our sense of what we deserve emerges from childhood. When we carry about with us a legacy of not quite having a right to satisfaction, the good will of others may prove bewildering and inspire unconscious attempts to repel or disappoint it self-destructively. It will simply feel more normal and therefore comfortable to be disliked or ignored.

Or we may, when we were younger, have been exposed to exceptionally brutal disappointments at a time when we were too fragile to withstand them. Perhaps we hoped our parents would stay together and they didn't. Or we hoped our father would eventually come back from another country and he stayed away. Perhaps we dared to love an adult and, after a period of happiness, they swiftly and oddly changed their attitude and let us down. Somewhere in our characters, a deep association has been forged between hope and danger, along with a corresponding preference to live quietly with disappointment, rather than more freely with hope.

The solution is to remind ourselves that we can, despite our fears, survive the loss of hope. We are no longer those who suffered the disappointments responsible for our present timidity. The conditions that forged our caution are no longer those of adult reality. The unconscious mind may, as is its wont, be reading the present through the lenses of decades ago, but what we fear will happen has in truth already happened;

we are projecting into the future a catastrophe that belongs to a past we have not had the chance to fathom and mourn adequately.

We are suffering from an enduring localised immaturity: an archaic part of us remains as it was when we were young. It has not been able to grow and shed its terrors. The intensity of fear is based on the idea that we can only bring childhood resources to the problem. We still feel the same age as when we met a horrendous loss.

But in fact, we're big now. We have the capacity to cope very well. Should this relationship fail, should this job not work out, should our hopes not be met, we'll be sad for a while but won't be destroyed. We are not in as much danger as the primitive part of the mind thinks – and as we once were. The catastrophe is behind us.

If happiness has not been a big part of our history, we should be conscious of how hard or unnerving it may prove to get close to some of the things we truly want.

See also: Inner Voices.

¶ Sentimentality

Sentimentality is a permanent temptation of our minds, resulting from squeamishness around excessively unpleasant evidence and ideas.

It is sentimentality that leads us to think that adults couldn't really abuse the children who are in their care; that it would be impossible for humans to harm something as large as the earth; that capitalism couldn't have major errors in its functioning; that expensive family holidays will go well; that birthdays are always going to be fun; and that young couples who look attractive and sweet can be assured of happiness, especially after a lavish wedding ceremony.

We're sentimental not from a lack of intelligence, but from a lack of courage, because the truth is simply so hard to bear.

In response to sentimentality, it is tempting to force others to shed their illusions with a certain brutality, to become sharply cynical to counter the prevailing saccharine assumptions. This is rarely effective, however. By heightening the sense of threat, harshness simply invites a stronger reaction of defensive denial.

A major ambition of a good culture should be to make the truth bearable. It shouldn't blame us when we naturally resist reality; it should induct us to it with special care. Culture should understand that we have to be let down gently and that we need a lot of encouragement to take the full facts of existence on board. In a good culture, the darker things are not denied or flaunted; they are artfully and consolingly handled.

See Also: Cheerful Despair; Consolation; Jolliness; Pessimism; Premeditation; Resilience; Splitting and Integration.

¶ Service

Service refers to the urge to devote ourselves to the well-being of others through our work. Few of us explicitly view ourselves as being concerned with service. We are encouraged to think that we are primarily selfish creatures. But what is striking is the extent to which what we actually require from our working days is a sense that we are able either to increase the pleasure or decrease the suffering of others through our labour. When this feeling is unavailable, no amount of money may be able to compensate – and when it is very present, not even a negligible income can distract us.

Some work fits the requirement for service with ease: the nurse and the cardiac surgeon are in no doubt that they are of service. But there are less dramatic yet equally essential forms of service-related satisfaction to be found in a range of less obvious tasks: sanding someone's floor; making efficient toothpaste dispensers; clearing up the accounts; delivering letters; helping someone to improve their backhand.

When work is of service, we can trace a connection between the things we do and a modest but real contribution to the improvement of humankind. It would be rather simple if all we wanted from work was money. However, we want something far more ambitious and far more complicated: the feeling of having made a difference.

See also: Meaningful Work; Misemployment.

¶ Sex and Love

One of the great burdens that our Romantic culture has imposed upon long-term relationships is the idea that, if things are working as they should, love and sexual fulfilment must always fit neatly together.

This beautiful and hugely convenient idea raises a passionate hope that over many years two people will not only like and help one another, manage their domestic finances reasonably well, perhaps raise a family, have enjoyable holidays, understand one another's problems, schedule cleaning rotas, put up with each other's failings, see each other's parents and friends and pursue their careers in harmony, but they will also be devoted and exciting sexual partners, endlessly entwining and recombining, sometimes being gentle and slow, at others, brutal and urgent, travelling together on a shared, life-long erotic adventure.

It is this sublime idea that begins to torment us when – as is the case in almost every relationship – sex gradually becomes less intense and less frequent, more cautious and

S

more frustrating, more at odds with daily life and eventually more daunting as a prospect than reading a book, watching the news together or simply going to sleep. This can appear nothing short of a catastrophe, a sign of monstrous failure and very often a prelude to a break-up.

Yet the problem is not ours alone. It is simply that almost everything that can make love go well seems primed not to make sex go well, and vice versa. We are afflicted by a fundamental misalignment in the qualities of character and spirit required by good sex on the one hand and successful love on the other.

A relationship cannot survive in the long term without tenderness, soberness, practical intelligence and selective resignation. We have to carefully fathom another's motives, explain our moods, overcome hurts and sulks and assume a mantle of predictability.

Sex, on the other hand, in its most dramatic, thrilling versions, demands that we be heedless, decadent, perhaps cruel or untenably submissive. It can involve the crudest language and moments of beautiful, tender degradation.

In having to suffer from feelings of inadequacy around what happens in long-term love, we are the victims of major cultural failure: the failure of our surrounding culture to continually stress a realistic picture of an unavoidable tension between two crucial yet incompatible themes of existence.

In a wiser world, we would collectively admit that the very rare cases where love and sex did run together were astonishing exceptions with no relevance to the majority of lives. We would instead learn to pay admiring attention to those who had accepted with a reasonable show of dignity and grace that the natural price of long-term togetherness is a decline in the quality and frequency of sexual contact – and that this is, in many cases, a price worth paying.

See also: Infidelity; Long-Term Love; Normality; Polyamory; Secrets in Love; Sexual Fetishes; Sexual Liberation.

¶ Sexual Fetishes

Sexual fetishes are points – parts of the body, clothes, scenarios – where our erotic excitement reaches a pitch. They are commonly frowned upon and understood as either entirely mysterious or very sinister. They are neither. They are closely connected with the deepest strands in our personalities and reflect some of our most sincere commitments and beliefs.

The things that turn us on are, at heart, almost always solutions to things we fear and symbols of how we'd like things to be. They are small moments of Utopia enacted around points of our sexuality.

Consider, for example, the fetish for rough sex. Modern life demands extreme politeness and restraint. We have to keep our bossiness in check. But in our hearts, we might like to be very forceful occasionally, exploring a demanding and insistent side to us. We would like sometimes to enforce absolute obedience on all those who defy us. But in the real world, of course, this is made difficult by the fact that very few people trust us to exercise such power; we simply are not able to rise to the status that would allow us to exercise power as we would want.

In our fetish, we dream that someone else will acknowledge our strength and wisdom, will recognise our talents and will put us wholly in charge of them. No more need for restraint, no more need to hold our tongue. In the sexual fetish, someone puts themselves in our hands, as we always hoped might happen. This is an attempt to address the very delicate, and very real problem, of when one is right to exercise decisive power over another person.

Or consider the fetish for outdoor sex. We easily become shy about the public realm; we sense that we have to be guarded, on our best behaviour, out there in the elevators, public plazas, shopping centres and garage forecourts of the world. Even nature is seen as quite hostile – a cold, dangerous place where enemies may set upon us.

S

So the longing arises that we could be as much at ease in the outdoors, in public and in nature, as we can be at home. It would be a solution to a kind of oppression to have sex in the elevator, in the library stacks, out near the river … Sex outdoors is pleasurable for the same reasons as picnics are: they are ways of taming the world by taking the domestic out into it. Any activity that has become linked to the indoors can be blissful when done outside because it symbolises a conquest of our anxieties – it is a way of imagining being more at home in the world than we normally can be.

One can analyse almost any fetish (shyness, cardigans, flat shoes, boots, cigars, stockings, striped socks, etc.) and find similar structures: an anxiety and a corresponding longing, to which an erotic charge has become connected. Looked at like this, sexual scenarios can be explained to ourselves – and, crucially, to other people in our lives – in rational, sensible terms.

By talking like this, we can hope that sexual fetishes will become a little less shameful and a little less threatening – and our erotic solutions a bit more reasonable and, in their own way, a lot more logical.

See also: Sex and Love; Sexual Liberation.

¶ Sexual Liberation

We tend to believe that we live in an era of sexual liberation. We tell ourselves a story of progress, from the repression of the Victorians and the religious fanatics to the openness of modernity. There are indeed some signs of genuine change. Stand-up comics can make jokes about masturbation, women's sexual appetites have been recognised, bathrooms are designed to feel airy and open. Yet the notion that we are liberated causes us problems all of its own, because it brings with it the assumption that hang-ups and awkwardness can no longer legitimately exist.

In truth, of course, true liberation remains a radically unfinished project; 'unfinished' because we continue to struggle to admit key things about who we are from a sexual perspective. This becomes especially painful around relationships, given that, for many of us, the dream of love is that we will at last be able to admit to who we are sexually without embarrassment. Yet the reality is more awkward. We frequently find ourselves facing an apparent choice between being honest and being liked.

The choice is not good for us. The sense that we need to hide, deny and bury away key elements of who we are is not, overall, very good for us. When we repress things that are important, they make themselves heard in other ways. As psychoanalysis has revealed, the 'dirty' parts of ourselves can show up disguised as greed, harsh opinions, bad temper, alcoholism or other forms of risky, damaging behaviour. There is a high price to disavowing powerful parts of ourselves: our sexuality can become split from our more enduring relationships. We may lose potency and desire with those we love, so unacceptable does our sexuality appear to be to us, so at odds with our higher feelings. Freud first noted this pattern in early 20th-century Vienna: 'Where they love, they cannot desire. Where they desire, they cannot love.'

True sexual liberation or self-acceptance doesn't have to mean abandoning all control or deliberately flaunting our less elevated needs at every turn. We don't have to fully embrace every impulse: we still need privacy and bathroom doors; we just need to be able to admit in an unfrightened way to ourselves and at points to our partners who we really are.

The core point of true liberation is to reduce the unfair and debilitating burden of shame with which we continue to wrestle only too often. Our goal should be to adopt a mature perspective on our own sexuality and to increase opportunities for moments of courageous and relationship-enhancing honesty.

See also: Better Porn; Sex and Love; Sexual Fetishes.

¶ Shyness

Shyness is a consequence of a paralysing and yet always mistaken impression of the difference between ourselves and other people. In the kindest way, it is a symptom of the provincialism of our minds.

At shy moments, we are overwhelmed by a sense of the otherness of others. They are all women, and we are a man. They are rich and we are poor. They are from the north, and we're from the south. The obstacles appear insurmountable.

The way past them is to recall that each of us has both a local and a universal identity. The local identity comprises age, gender, skin colour, sexuality, social background, career and religion. But this is not the limit of who we are. Within our universal identity is the fact that we all have problematic families, have all been disappointed, have all been idiotic, have all been loved, have all been hated, have all had problems around sex, have all had anxieties – and will all bleed if we are pricked. The last point alludes to Shylock's haunting plea in Shakespeare's The Merchant of Venice:

> I am a Jew. Hath not a Jew eyes? Hath not a Jew hands, organs, dimensions, senses, affections, passions? Fed with the same food, hurt with the same weapons, subject to the same diseases, healed by the same means, warmed and cooled by the same winter and summer as a Christian is? If you prick us, do we not bleed? If you tickle us, do we not laugh? If you poison us, do we not die?

Shylock's words are relevant not only to a prejudiced audience. They are of huge potential benefit to the shy as well. However unbelievable it may seem at nervous moments, we invariably have much in common with any member of our species. It is no coincidence that Shakespeare had read and absorbed the writings of the Roman playwright Terence, who is remembered for his declaration: *Homo sum, humani nihil a me alienum puto* ('I am human, nothing human is foreign to me').

At times when we cannot help but doubt this concept, when we can readily see no echo of any of our concerns in the faces of others, we must make a social leap of faith:

Even though the person I see in front of me seems alien in a hundred ways, even though I can currently notice no points of similarity, this cannot be true. There will, and has to be, a shared universal humanity, which it is within my powers to discover.

See also: Normality; Psychological Asymmetry; Sane Insanity; Universal Love; Warmth.

¶ Small Pleasures

Small pleasures – which comprise such elements as a warm bath, a slice of fresh bread, a conversation with a close friend or a good night of sleep – lack prestige or social support. Our age believes in big pleasures. We have inherited a Romantic suspicion of the ordinary (which is taken to be mediocre, dull and uninspiring) and work with a corresponding assumption that things that are unique, hard to find, exotic, or unfamiliar are naturally fitted to delight us more. We subtly like high prices. If something is cheap or free, it's a little harder to appreciate. We are mostly focused on large schemes that we hope will deliver substantial enjoyment: marriage, career, travel and the purchase of a house.

S

The approach isn't wholly wrong, but it unwittingly exhibits a vicious and unhelpful bias against the cheap, the easily available, the ordinary, the familiar and the small-scale.

The paradoxical aspect of pleasure is how promiscuous it proves to be. It doesn't neatly collect in the most expensive boutiques. It can refuse to stick with us on grand holidays. It is remarkably vulnerable to emotional trouble, sulks and casual bad moods.

A pleasure may look very minor – eating a fig, whispering in bed in the dark, talking to a grandparent, or scanning through old photos – and yet be anything but. If properly grasped and elaborated upon, these sorts of activities may be among the most moving and satisfying we can have.

Appreciating what is to hand isn't a defence of failure; it isn't an attack on ambition. But there is no point in chasing the future until and unless we are attuned to the modest moments and things that are available to us already.

The smallness of a pleasure isn't really an assessment of how much it has to offer us: it is a reflection of how many good things the world unfairly neglects. A small pleasure is a great pleasure in waiting; it is a true source of joy that has not yet received the collective acknowledgment it is due.

See also: Domesticity; Getting an Early Night; Rock Appreciation; Quiet Life, The; Water Towers.

¶ Snobbery

Snobbery is a method of judging people not according to the totality of their being, but with reference to a punishingly narrow range of criteria.

In the modern world, the operative criteria of judgement are work and money. In the past, snobs might have wanted to know a person's family lineage; now, they are focused on what they do for a living, and then judge their entire worth upon this piece of information. One of the first questions that a snob may ask of a stranger at a party is, 'And what do you do?' According to how the question is answered, they will either grow solicitous and animated, or will abandon the unfortunate low-status figure to a solitary fate by the nuts.

The more prevalent snobbery happens to be, the more our income and status start to matter. We are not being materialistic; we simply recognise that certain emotional rewards (a feeling of being valued, respected, honoured) will only be available to us via material goods. It isn't the material goods we want so much as the 'love' that results from their possession.

In principle, the snob is asking an important question: how impressive or good is a person? But they are brutally misguided in how they set about answering it. For snobs, it is the already acclaimed and already successful who are the only ones worthy of respect. There is no room to imagine that someone might be clever, kind or good, and yet have somehow been entirely overlooked by society. Snobs don't sign The Beatles, don't invest in the startup iteration of Google or Apple, don't give the time of day to the taxi driver who might one day be the president, or to the old lady in a woolly hat who is writing the great novel of the 21st century – or might simply be a rather lovely person.

The true answer to snobbery is not to say that there is no such thing as a better or worse person, but to insist that 'better or worse' exist in constantly unexpected places and carry none of the outward signs of distinction. Because we are such poor judges of the worth of others, our ultimate duty remains to be kind, good, curious and imaginative about pretty much everyone who might ever cross our path.

See also: Day of Judgement; Love as Generosity; Meritocracy.

¶ Specialisation

The modern economy demands, and rewards, specialisation. The reason why was first elaborated at the end of the 18th century by the Scottish philosopher Adam Smith. In *The Wealth of Nations* (1776), Smith explained how specialisation – what he termed the 'division of labour' – decisively increases collective productivity. In a society where everyone does everything, only a small number of shoes, houses, nails, bushels of wheat, horse bridles and cart wheels are ever produced, as no one ends up especially good or efficient at producing anything. But if people specialise in just one small area (making rivets, shaping spokes, manufacturing rope, bricklaying, etc.), they become much faster and more efficient and the overall level of production is greatly increased. By focusing our efforts, our societies grow wealthier and better supplied with the goods they need. It is a tribute to the world Smith foresaw that we have ended up with highly specialised job titles such as Senior Packaging & Branding Designer, Intake and Triage Clinician, Research Centre Manager, Risk and Internal Audit Controller and Transport Policy Consultant – in other words, tiny cogs in giant efficient machines.

Despite all this, we are at grave risk of getting bored. Deep in our hearts, most of us long to be wide-ranging, endlessly curious generalists. We can understand the origins of this restlessness when we look at childhood. As children, we were allowed to do so much. In a single Saturday morning, we might put on an extra jumper and imagine being an Arctic explorer, then have brief stints as an architect making a Lego house, a rock star making up an anthem about cornflakes and an inventor working out how to speed up colouring-in by gluing four felt-tip pens together. We'd put in a few minutes as a member of an emergency rescue team, then we'd try out being a pilot brilliantly landing a cargo plane on the rug in the corridor; we'd perform a life-saving operation on a knitted rabbit, and finally we'd find employment as a sous-chef helping to make a ham and cheese sandwich for lunch.

Each one of these 'games' might have been the beginning of a career, yet we had to settle on only a single option, done repeatedly over fifty years. We are so much more than the world of work ever allows us to be. We have chosen to make work pay more rather than be more interesting. It's a sombre thought, but a consoling one too. Our suffering is painful but has a curious dignity to it, because it does not uniquely affect us as individuals. It applies as much to the CEO as to the intern, to the artist as much as to the accountant. Everyone could have found so many versions of happiness that will elude them. In suffering in this way, we are participating in the common human lot. Whatever we do, parts of our potential will have to go undeveloped and die without having had the chance to come to full maturity – for the sake of the genuine benefits of focus and specialisation.

See also: Communism; Meaningful Work.

¶ Splitting and Integration

The pioneering mid-20th-century Viennese psychoanalyst Melanie Klein drew attention to something very dramatic that happens in the minds of babies during feeding sessions with their mothers. When feeding goes well, the baby is blissfully happy and sees mummy as 'good'. But if, for whatever reason, the feeding process is difficult, the baby can't grasp that it is dealing with the same person it liked a lot only a few hours ago. It splits off from the actual mother a second, 'bad' version, whom it deems to be a separate, hateful individual, responsible for deliberately frustrating its wishes, and in the process, protecting the image of the good mother in its mind.

Gradually, if things go well, there follows a long and difficult process by which the child integrates these two different people and comes, sadly but realistically, to grasp that there

S

is no ideal, 'perfect' mummy – just one person who is usually lovely but can also be cross, busy, tired, who can make mistakes, and be very interested in other people.

It may have been a long time since we were being fed as babies, but the tendency to 'split' those close to us is always there, for we never fully outgrow our childhood selves. In adult life, we may fall deeply in love and split off an ideal version of someone, in whom we see no imperfections and whom we adore without limit. Yet we may suddenly and violently turn against the partner (or a celebrity or a politician) whose good qualities once impressed us, the moment we discover the slightest thing that disturbs or frustrates us in them. We may conclude that they cannot really be good since they have made us suffer.

We may find it extremely hard to accept that the same person might be very nice and good in some ways and strikingly disappointing in others. The bad version can appear to destroy the good one, although these are really just different and connected aspects of one complex person.

To cope with the conflict between hope and reality, our culture should teach us good integration skills, prompting us to accept what is imperfect in ourselves and others. We should be gently reminded that no one we can love will ever satisfy us completely, but that it is never worth hating them on that score alone. We should move from the naivety and rage of Splitting to the mature wisdom of Integration.

See also: Being 'Good'; Cheerful Despair; Crushes; Good Enough; Kintsugi; Melancholy; Sentimentality; Weakness of Strength; Wisdom.

¶ State Broadcasting

Most modern states possess a nationally owned broadcaster – and most wonder what it is actually for. Typically the argument is that it should provide worthy but unpopular programming that the free market wouldn't support.

But there's another, more impressive, purpose they could have: to improve the psychology of the nation. A large, arguably even the largest, share of the issues undermining advanced nations are 'psychological' at their root; that is, they have to do with our minds, with our deeper patterns of thinking and feeling. These problems include family breakdown, domestic violence, poor parenting, alcoholism, drug addiction, obesity, depression, chronic anxiety, delinquency and loneliness. Taken together, these issues directly – and indirectly – cost national governments a massive share of their annual national budgets. Currently, there is no easy way for governments to address any of these problems.

This is where the tantalising opportunity lies. Just within reach of most governments, available for no extra money, stands the most powerful lever imaginable: the state broadcaster. Broadcasting is the single most effective way of changing mentalities, dramatically more helpful than a book, leaflet or class. Revolutionaries have always known this; it's why they have always driven their tanks to the TV station first.

In order to stand any chance of addressing national psychological ills, it is key to get into people's minds on a huge scale, with charm and skill, at regular, repeated intervals. The challenge wouldn't be (as now) to make the odd unpopular programme about important things, but to turn out consistently compelling work that points to the resolution of the most damaging patterns of behaviour.

With enough creativity applied, public broadcasting could do more to cure the troubles of nations than the police force,

S

social services and the drugs squad combined. A huge opportunity is at hand, waiting for the necessary political will, intellectual focus and creative talent to develop.

See also: Changing the World; Good Nationalism; Seduction; Utopia.

¶ Sublime, The

The Sublime refers to an experience of vastness (of space, age, time) beyond calculation or comprehension – a sense of awe we might feel before an ocean, a glacier, the earth from a plane or a starry sky.

In the presence of the Sublime, we are made to feel desperately small. In most of life, a sense of our smallness is experienced as a humiliation – when it happens, for example, at the hands of a professional enemy or a concierge. But the impression of smallness that unfolds in the presence of the Sublime has an oddly uplifting and profoundly redemptive effect. We are granted an impression of our complete nullity and insignificance in a grander scheme, which relieves us from an often oppressive sense of the seriousness of all our ambitions and desires and of all our rivals and heroes. We welcome being put back in our place and not having to take ourselves quite so seriously – not least because the agent doing so is as noble and awe-inspiring as a ten-thousand-year-old ice sheet or a volcano on the surface of Mars.

Things that have up until now been looming in our minds (what's gone wrong with the Seville office, a colleague's cold behaviour, the disagreement about patio furniture) is usefully cut down in size. Local, immediate sorrows are reduced; none of our troubles, disappointments or hopes has very much significance for a time. Everything that happens to us, or that we do, is of no consequence whatever from the point of view of the universe. We are granted a perspective within which our own concerns are mercifully irrelevant.

Bits of our egoism and pride seem less impressive. We may be moved to be more tolerant, less wrapped up in our own concerns. We're reminded of our fragility and transient occupation of the world, which can move us to focus on what's genuinely important, while there is still time. The Sublime foregrounds a sense of equality, which we can otherwise find it hard to hold onto. In the face of vast things, the grades of human status lose meaning. The CEO and the intern are equally transient arrangements of atoms.

Our reversals matter less as well. We become more alive to the impersonal, implacable forces that erode all aspects of nature and, hence, all our lives. Like the cliffs under the pressure of the raging oceans, our plans will collapse and fail. Our griefs are universal and unavoidable. The intense burden of the unfairness of existence is reduced.

Crucially, the Sublime isn't just an idea; it's a piece of applied philosophy experienced via the senses. The mere idea of our own littleness won't impact upon us just as an abstract proposition. We have to feel it; we have to stand at the edge of the ocean with the wind raging about us or see the Singapore Straits from thirty thousand feet at dawn. The importance of a sensory impression reveals a general truth about how our minds work: pure ideas are feeble tools for affecting human conduct; we can too easily shrug off words. This is why art and travel are ideal resources of culture. At their best, they integrate thought and feeling: the good idea they are seeking to teach us is delivered in the way we need – wrapped up in powerful sensory emotions.

We need not just the idea of cliffs; for philosophy to work its proper effect, we need regularly to take the whole of our-selves out to them.

See also: Akrasia; Animals; Nature.

¶ Success at School vs. Success in Life

Given how long we spend in schools of various kinds, and the intense efforts we often make to obtain good grades in them, it is bewildering and deeply counter-intuitive how often success at school does not automatically translate into success in life: the star student may move into a good-sounding job, but then not flourish; the person who couldn't pass their exams may end up running the business (or, as importantly, may form a long-term, contented relationship).

If we examine the current dominant idea of education, the disconnect is not surprising. Success at school hinges on attitudes and mental habits that have little to offer when we face the challenges on which success in life depends.

The root of the problem is that school curricula are not reverse-engineered from fulfilled adult lives in the here and now. They don't start by asking what skills and knowledge actually serve us in adulthood and devote themselves to nurturing star pupils in those areas. Instead, schools are typically fixated on several unhelpful ideas: that primarily you have to learn what is known already, rather than develop the capacity to solve problems to which no handy solution yet exists; that it is the intellect that needs to be trained, whereas it is the quality of our emotional intelligence that will make the biggest difference in our professional and personal relationships; that the teacher knows and you don't, whereas in the rest of life, people in positions of authority may well be deeply mistaken in their views; that longer is better, though brevity, wit and memorable one-liners carry more weight everywhere else.

Schools teach us to redeploy rather than originate ideas; to seek permission; to meet rather than change expectations; to imagine that those in charge know what they are doing rather than guessing one can do better. Schools teach us anything other than the two skills that really determine the quality of adult life: knowing how to choose the right job, and knowing how to form satisfactory relationships.

That said, it isn't the case that all we need to do to succeed at life is to flunk school. A good life requires us to do two very tricky things: be an extremely good boy or girl for twenty years, and simultaneously never really to believe in the long-term validity or seriousness of what we're being asked to study. We need to be outwardly entirely obedient while inwardly intelligently and committedly rebellious.

See also: Emotional Intelligence; School of Life, The; Wisdom.

¶ Suicide

One of the most surprising aspects about one of the saddest of all human possibilities is that the suicide rate goes up markedly the richer and more developed a society becomes. We might expect suicide rates to vary across time and place, but not to increase alongside developments in wealth, comfort and security. That we should be unwittingly creating nations in which more of us end up killing ourselves appears to negate the whole purpose of economic growth.

Nevertheless, the disturbing connection was first identified towards the end of the 19th century by the French sociologist Emile Durkheim, and has continued to be noted ever since. The suicide rate of a less developed country like the Democratic Republic of the Congo is a fraction of the rate of a developed nation like South Korea. The crucial factor behind people's decision to end their lives is not really wealth or poverty. As Durkheim discovered, it is the extent to which the surrounding culture ascribes responsibility for failure to individuals or else maintains a faith that poor luck or divine intervention are to blame instead.

It so happens that as societies become modern and industrialised, they very frequently give up their beliefs in demons and gods and start instead to trust in a meritocratic, individualistic

S

philosophy that suggests to people that their fate is always in their own hands. This may sound generous, but it carries an immense psychological burden: when failures occur, the individual is held entirely responsible for them. Reversals start to seem like a horrendous judgement on one's worth and a public humiliation from which there may, at the extreme, seem no escape other than self-annihilation.

But suicide is merely the most extreme symptom of a more general sense of personal responsibility. It isn't the wealth of a nation we should blame; it is its ideology.

There are two big cultural ideas that may help to mitigate the pressures upon us: luck and tragedy. To believe in luck is accurately to observe that merit and success are never reliably aligned: one may be a fool and win, or a virtuous person and fail. If we fully internalise and widely share the notion of luck, then the shame of failure will be greatly reduced, and our agony along with it. We will be able to admit, publicly and to ourselves, that decent people can fail in their outward circumstances and that professional success isn't the only, or even the crucial, marker of the merit of human beings.

Tragedy, as it originated in Ancient Greece, is the story of a capable and intelligent person who happens to make a small mistake, which leads to appalling consequences. The point of presenting such stories in very public ways (the entire community had to attend Greek festivals) was to continually renew acquaintance with a hugely important idea: that one can be a likeable, even admirable, person and end up in an utterly desperate situation. Tragedy is the careful telling of how disaster can come into the lives of people like (or even a bit nicer than) us. They – and hence we – are always deserving of compassion rather than contempt.

Durkheim knew that it is not prosperity by itself that increases the suicide rate. The toxic element is an unwittingly cruel culture that assigns a high burden of responsibility to us, while seeming to deny the truth that chance and tragedy will always affect our destinies.

The real solution to a high suicide rate lies in an unexpected place: an ideology that firmly reminds us that we are never the sole authors of our destinies.

See also: Artistic Sympathy; Equality and Envy; Luck; Meritocracy; Tragedy.

¶ Sulking

Sulking combines a powerful symbolic articulation of anger with an intense desire not to communicate what one is angry about. One both desperately needs to be understood and yet is profoundly committed to not making it easy for another person to understand one.

The stance is no coincidence. One remains silent and furiously gnomic because having to spell out the offence another has caused feels contrary to the spirit of love, interpreted in a Romantic sense: if the other requires an explanation, it is proof they are not worthy of being granted one. After all, true love should be about mutual speedy intuition, not laborious articulation.

In a sense, it is an odd privilege to be the recipient of a sulk, for one tends to fall into a sulk only with people whom one feels should understand one, in whom one has placed a high degree of trust, and yet who appear to have broken the contract of the relationship. We would never dare to storm out of a room, call someone a shit and stay silent the rest of the evening in an upstairs room unless one was with a partner whom one believed had a profound capacity to understand one, which they had – strangely, probably out of spite – chosen not to use on this occasion. It is one of the stranger gifts of love.

S

Sulking pays homage to a beautiful, yet in practice catastrophic, Romantic ideal of love: that of being understood without needing to speak. At a deep level, the structure of the sulk reveals a debt to earliest childhood. In the womb, we never had to explain what we needed. Food and comfort simply came. If we had the privilege of being relatively well parented, some of that idyll may have continued in our first years. We didn't have to make our every need known; someone guessed for us. They saw through our tears, our inarticulacy, our confusions, and found the explanations when we didn't have the ability to verbalise them. The sulker continues to want to be interpreted the way they once were.

The cure is a dose of pessimism. We should be reminded of the unfairness of wanting every aspect of our souls to be grasped without us needing to say a word. It is not necessarily an insult to be misunderstood and called upon to communicate. When our lovers fail to fathom us and unwittingly barge into our more tender sides, it isn't an immediate sign that they are heartless. It may merely be that we have grown a little too committed to not teaching them about who we are.

See also: Teaching and Learning.

T

¶ Teaching and Learning

Teaching and learning are the two central emotional skills we need for life among other humans. Considered properly, teaching – by which we mean the business of getting an important idea from one mind into another – is vital in any couple, office or family we'll ever belong to. Every one of us, whatever our occupation, needs to become a good teacher, for our lives constantly require us to deliver crucial information with grace and effectiveness into the deep minds of others. Furthermore, we also need the humility required by the student role: we need to recall how little we know; we need to acknowledge how generally unpleasant it is to have to take anything new on board; and we need to admit how tempting it is to blame the teacher rather than confront their message.

Most of us probably started off by being quite bad teachers, with tendencies to get annoyed by the fact that another person doesn't know something yet – even though we have never told them what it might be. Certain ideas can seem so important to us, we can't imagine that others don't already know them. We suspect they may be deliberately upsetting us by pretending not to have a clue. This attitude makes it unlikely that what we actually have to teach will make its way successfully into the other person's head. Good teaching starts with the idea that ignorance is not a defect of the individual we're instructing; it's the consequence of never having been properly taught. The fault only ever belongs with the people who haven't done enough to get the needed ideas into others' heads – in other words, with you.

T

The more we need other people to know something, the less we may be able to secure the calm frame of mind that is indispensable if we are to have a chance of conveying it to them effectively. The possibility that they won't quickly understand a point that matters immensely to us can drive us into an agitated fury – the very worst state in which to conduct any lesson. By the time we've started to insult our so-called pupil, to shout, call them a blockhead or a fool, the lesson is plainly over. No one has ever learnt anything under conditions of humiliation. Paradoxically, the best sort of teachers can bear the possibility that what they have to teach will not be understood. It is this slightly detached, slightly pessimistic approach that stands the best chance of generating the relaxed frame of mind essential to successful pedagogy.

Good teachers are also good students. They know that everyone has a lot to learn and everyone has something important to impart to others. We should never become incensed if someone is trying to teach us something. We should never want to be liked just as we are. Only a perfect being would be committed to their own status quo. For the rest of us, good learning and teaching are the only ways to ensure we have a chance of developing into slightly better versions of ourselves.

See also: Love as Education; Love Me as I Am; Nagging; Procrastination; Seduction; Sulking; Teasing.

¶ Teasing

Teasing done with affection and skill is a profound human accomplishment. There is nasty teasing, of course, in which we pick away at a sore spot in someone's life. But there is a genuinely valuable affectionate version, generous and loving, which feels good to be on the receiving end of.

All of us become a bit unbalanced in one way or another: too serious, too gloomy, too jokey. We all benefit from being tugged back towards a healthier mean by a well-aimed, tenderly delivered tease. The good teaser latches onto and responds to our distinctive quirks and is compassionately constructive about trying to reconnect us with our better selves – not by delivering a stern lesson, but by helping us to notice our excesses and laugh at them. We sense the teaser trying, with love, to give us a useful shove in a good (and secretly welcome) direction.

The best teasing remarks emerge from genuine insights into who we are. A person has studied us, put their finger on a struggle that's going on in us and has taken the part of the highest – but currently under-supported – side of us. This feels so good because, only too often, others simply don't see past the forbidding or off-putting front we assume for the world; they have no imagination to detect the kinder self beneath the tricky surface. They simply think we are gloomy, stern, angry or obsessed. The teaser does us the favour of recognising that the dominant front doesn't tell the whole story.

Teasing is a subtle, powerful mode of teaching. It builds on a hugely important insight about human beings: criticism of any kind is exceptionally hard to absorb; we are slow and reluctant learners, with well-observed tendencies to ignore and turn against those who try to lecture us. By amusingly exaggerating our exaggerations, teasing combines criticism with charm. The negative point is real, but it is carefully wrapped in kindness and disguised as entertainment – and is therefore much easier to take on board. It seduces us into virtue. ('If you want to tell people the truth, make them laugh, otherwise they'll kill you', knew George Bernard Shaw.)

Perhaps the most instructive question we can ask – the one that teaches us most about the value of affectionate teasing and of the path we still need to take towards emotional maturity – is simply: what do I need to be teased about?

See also: Teaching and Learning; Universal Love.

¶ Tragedy

Our fear of failure would not be so great were it not for an awareness of how often failure tends to be harshly viewed and interpreted by others. We fear not just poverty; we're terrified of mockery and ridicule.

But there is one art form in particular that, since its inception, has dedicated itself to recounting stories of great failure without recourse to mockery or judgement. While not absolving people of responsibility for their actions, its achievement has been to offer to those involved in catastrophes – disgraced statesmen, murderers, the bankrupt, emotional compulsives – a level of sympathy owed, but rarely paid, to every human.

Tragic art began in the theatres of Ancient Greece in the 6th century BCE. It followed a hero, usually a high-born one, a king or a famous warrior, from prosperity and acclaim to ruin and shame, through some error of his own. The way the story was told was likely to leave audience members at once hesitant to condemn the hero for what had befallen him and humbled by recognising how easily they too might be ruined if they were ever in a situation similar to the hero's. The tragedy would leave them sorrowful before the difficulties of leading a good life and modest before those who had failed at the undertaking.

If a newspaper, with its language of perverts and weirdoes, failures and losers, lies at one end of the spectrum of understanding, then it is tragedy that lies at the other – attempting to build bridges between the guilty and the apparently blameless, challenging our ordinary conceptions of responsibility, standing as the most psychologically sophisticated, most respectful account of how a human being may be dishonoured, without at the same time forfeiting the right to be heard.

The tragedian draws us close to an almost unbearable truth: that every folly or blindness of which a human being has been guilty can be traced back to aspects of our own nature; that we bear within ourselves the whole of the human condition, in its worst and best aspects, so that we too might be capable of anything under the right (or very wrong) circumstances. Once an audience has been brought close to this fact, they may willingly dismount from their high horses and feel their powers of sympathy and humility enhanced; they may accept how easily their own lives could be shattered if certain of their more regrettable character traits, which had until then led to no serious accident, were one day to come into contact with a situation that allowed these flaws unlimited and catastrophic reign.

That the legendary failed characters of art seem noble to us has little to do with their qualities per se and almost everything to do with the way we have been taught to consider them by their creators and chroniclers.

See also: Art for Art's Sake; Artistic Sympathy; Consolation; Day of Judgement; Inner Voices; Luck; Original Sin; Suicide; Universal Love.

¶ Transference

Transference is a psychological phenomenon whereby a situation in the present elicits from us a response – generally extreme, intense or rigid in nature – that we cobbled together in childhood to meet a threat that we were at that time too vulnerable, immature and inexperienced to cope with properly. We are drawing upon an old defence mechanism to respond to what feels like a very familiar threat.

In most of our pasts, when our powers of comprehension and control were not yet properly developed, we faced difficulties so great that our capacities for poise and trust suffered grievous damage. In relation to certain issues, we were warped. We grew up preternaturally nervous, suspicious, hostile, sad, closed, furious or touchy, and are at risk of becoming so once

T

again whenever life puts us in a situation that is distantly evocative of our earlier troubles.

The unconscious mind is slow to realise that things have changed in the outer world and is quick to mistake one person for another, twenty years ago for now, seeming to judge only by the crudest of correspondences.

Transference generally happens without us knowing it. We think we are responding to the present while in fact being guided by a pattern from the past. We carry years behind us that we have forgotten about and that we aren't in a position to talk others through in a manner that would win us sympathy and understanding. We can easily just come across as mean or mad.

The concept of transference provides a vantage point on some of the most frustrating behaviours that any of us ever generate. It allows us to feel sympathy for other people where we might have felt only irritation. A wiser culture would teach us that transference is normal. Recognising that one is doing it oneself is not an admission of unusual idiocy; it's an instance of mature self-knowledge.

See also: Emotional Education; Emotional Scepticism; Faulty Walnut, The.

¶ Transitional Object

Between the ages of around one and twelve, many children manifest a deep attachment to a stuffed soft object, normally shaped into a bear, a rabbit or – less often – a penguin. The depth of the relationship can be extraordinary. The child sleeps with it, talks to it, cries in front of it and tells it things they would never tell anyone else. What's truly remarkable is that the animal looks after its owner, addressing them in a tone of unusual maturity and kindness. It might, in a crisis, urge the child not to worry and to look forward to better times in the future. Naturally, the animal's character is entirely made up. The animal is simply something invented, or brought to life, by one part of the child in order to look after the other.

The English psychoanalyst Donald Winnicott was the first person to write seriously and with sensitivity about the business of stuffed animals. He called them 'transitional objects'. In a paper from the early 1960s, Winnicott described a boy of six, whose parents had been abusive to him, becoming very connected to a small animal his grandmother had given him. Every night, he would have a dialogue with the animal, would hug him close to his chest and shed a few tears into his stained and greying soft fur. It was his most precious possession, for which he would have given up everything else. As the boy summarised the situation to Winnicott: 'No one else can understand me like bunny can.'

What fascinated Winnicott here was that it was the boy who had invented the rabbit, given him his identity, his voice and his way of addressing him. The boy was speaking to himself – via the bunny – in a voice filled with an otherwise all too rare compassion and sympathy.

Although it sounds a little odd, speaking to ourselves is common practice throughout our lives. Often, when we do so, the tone is harsh and punitive. We upbraid ourselves for being losers, time-wasters or perverts. But, as Winnicott knew, mental well-being depends on having to hand a repertoire of more gentle, forgiving and hopeful inner voices. To keep going, there are moments when one side of the mind needs to say to the other that the criticism is enough, that it understands, that this could happen to anyone, that one could not have known. It is this kind of indispensable benevolent voice that the child first starts to rehearse and exercise with the help of a stuffed animal.

In adolescence, animals tend to get put away. They become embarrassing, evoking a vulnerability we're keen to escape

T

from. But, to follow Winnicott, if our development has gone well, what was trialled in the presence of a stuffed animal should continue all of our lives, because, by definition, we will frequently be let down by the people around us, who won't be able to understand us, listen to our griefs and be kind to us in the manner we crave and require. Every healthy adult should therefore possess a capacity for self-nurture; that is, for retreating to a safe, secluded space and speaking in a tone that is gentle, encouraging and infinitely forgiving. That we don't formally label the understanding self 'white rabbit' or 'yellow bear' shouldn't obscure the debt that the nurturing adult self owes to its earlier embodiment in a furry toy.

A good adult life requires us to see the links between our strengths and our regressive states. Being properly mature demands a gracious accommodation with what can seem child-like, embarrassing or humiliatingly vulnerable. We should honour stuffed animals for what they really are: tools to help us on our first steps in the vital business of knowing how to look after ourselves.

See also: Inner Voices.

U

¶ Ugliness

Most of us are, to some extent, ugly. We should accept with Stoic good grace that personal appearance is simply one of the least democratic parts of life.

We tend to misunderstand how common ugliness is, in part because the images in the media always highlight the pretty ones. In truth, beauty is as rare as mass murder. The problem is that we tend to think there are far more murders than there are. Thanks to the media, it can feel as if everyone is knifing everyone else. We recognise symptoms of panic when the frequency of a bad thing is exaggerated. We don't yet recognise a similar hysteria when the frequency of a good thing gets exaggerated.

Fortunately, not everyone minds ugliness. The reason is simple. People learn about love from their parents; our elders provide the template for affection that comes into force when children grow up. Fortunately for the ugly, many parents who are kind and loving are also peculiar in looks. Many people, even very attractive ones, therefore grow up predisposed to think generously of not-so-perfect people. They are the physical types with whom they continue to associate comfort, safety and tenderness.

Ugliness is fascinatingly impervious to class and status. Given all the iniquities of the social system, it is some form of compensation that there should also be – alongside the near-feudal ranks of money and power – another hierarchy based on looks, in which a different elite is established and where the shop assistant may triumph over the CEO.

U

However random the distribution of appearance is today, time will – eventually – bring justice. No one ends up happy with how they look. For some, disenchantment may start at ten. For others it may require another forty years. It always happens.

The trouble with our culture is not so much that we love appearances, but that we allow too narrow a range of features to dominate our understanding of beauty. There is ultimately something attractive in everyone: perhaps an august bearing to the forehead, a melancholy sweetness in the eyes, a candour in the nose. We should broaden our criteria of where we find beauty. And hopefully someone, somewhere, will one day do the same for us.

See also: Appreciation; Normality; Resilience.

¶ Universal Love

The itinerant Galilean preacher known as Jesus not only spoke a great deal about love, but he also went on to advocate that we love some highly surprising people. At one point – described in chapter 7 of Luke's Gospel – he goes to a dinner party and a local prostitute turns up, much to the disgust of the hosts. But Jesus is friendly and sweet and defends her against everyone else's criticism. In a way that shocks the other guests, he insists that she is a good person at heart.

There's another story (in Matthew, chapter 8) where Jesus is approached by a man with leprosy. He's in a disgusting state. But Jesus isn't shocked; he reaches out his hand and touches the man. Despite the horrendous appearance, here is someone (in Jesus's eyes) entirely deserving of closeness and kindness. In a similar vein, at other times, Jesus conspicuously argues that tax collectors, thieves and adulterers are never to be thought of as outside the circle of love.

Many centuries after Jesus's death, the foremost medieval thinker Thomas Aquinas defined what Jesus was getting at in this way of talking about love: the person who truly understands love could love anyone, wrote Aquinas. In other words: true love isn't specific in its target; it doesn't fixate on particular qualities; it is open to all of humanity, even (and in a way especially) its less appealing examples.

This can sound like a deeply strange notion of what love is, for our background ideas about love tend to be closely tied to a dramatic experience: that of falling in love, finding one, very specific person immensely attractive, exciting and free of any failings or drawbacks. Love is, we feel, a response to the overt perfection of another person.

Yet – via some admittedly extreme examples – a very important aspect of love is being pushed to the fore in Jesus's vision. And we don't have to be Christian – that is, we don't have to believe that there's an afterlife or that Jesus was born to a virgin – to benefit from it.

At the heart of this kind of love is an effort to see beyond the outwardly unappealing surface of another human in search of the tender, interesting, scared and vulnerable person inside.

What we know as the 'work' of love is the emotional, imaginative labour required to peer behind an off-putting façade. Our minds tend to resist such a move. They follow well-worn grooves that feel at once familiar and justified. If someone has hurt us, we almost inevitably see them as mean, rather than, as might be the case, anxious or sad.

It takes quite a deliberate, taxing effort of the mind to move ourselves off our deeply established responses and to learn to see that everyone is, ultimately, fragile, hurt, damaged and deserving of love.

U

See also: Artistic Sympathy; Bad Taste; Charity of Interpretation; Inner Idiot, The; Love as Generosity; Other-as-Child; Shyness; Teasing; Tragedy; Weakness of Strength.

¶ Unprocessed Emotion

It is a quirk of our minds that not every emotion we carry is fully acknowledged, understood or even truly felt. There are feelings that exist in an 'unprocessed' form within us. A great many worries may remain disavowed and uninterpreted and manifest themselves as powerful, directionless anxiety. Under their sway, we may feel a compulsive need to remain busy, fear spending any time on our own, or cling to activities that ensure we don't meet what scares us head on (these might include internet pornography, tracking the news or exercising compulsively).

A similar kind of disavowal can go on around hurt. Someone may have abused our trust, made us doubt their kindness or violated our self-esteem, but we are driven to flee a frank recognition of an appalling degree of exposure and vulnerability. The hurt is somewhere inside, but on the surface, we adopt a brittle good cheer (jolliness being sadness that doesn't know itself), we numb ourselves chemically, or else adopt a carefully non-specific tone of cynicism that masks the specific wound that has been inflicted on us.

We pay dearly for our failure to 'process' our feelings. Our minds grow unoriginal from a background apprehension as to their contents. We grow depressed about everything because we cannot be sad about something. We can no longer sleep, insomnia being the revenge of all the many thoughts we have omitted to process in the day.

We need compassion for ourselves. We avoid processing emotions because what we feel is so contrary to our self-image, so threatening to our society's ideas of normality and so at odds with who we would like to be. An atmosphere conducive to processing would be one in which the difficulties of being human were warmly recognised and charitably accepted. We fail to know ourselves not out of laziness or casual neglect, but out of fear and shame.

Processing emotions requires good friends, deft therapists and ritual moments like Philosophical Meditation, in which our normal defences can safely be put aside and unfamiliar material ringfenced for investigation.

The outcome of processing our emotions is always an alleviation in our overall mood. But first we must pay for our self-awareness with a period of mourning in which we gradually acknowledge that, in some area or other, life is simply a lot sadder than we want it to be.

See also: Addiction; Insomnia; Jolliness; Philosophical Meditation; Self-Knowledge.

¶ Utopia

A Utopia is a picture of how things should be, as opposed to how they actually are. Utopian thinking involves wondering about a future altered for the better in a variety of ways. What if technology overcame the energy crisis? What if everyone were rich? What if we could fly in seconds to other planets?

A lot of utopian thinking currently focuses on technology and its power to overcome material and practical challenges. Yet some of the truly exciting developments we can ponder concern how we might alter the emotional sides of our lives.

We should allow ourselves to imagine a variety of ways in which our world could be transformed if our emotional needs were more clearly understood and given pride of place, if society were explicitly organised around the goal of eudaimonia and was dedicated to furnishing us with the psychological skills required for a flourishing life.

How might we reorganise marriage? How could schools be redesigned? How might working environments be reformed? What would the media be like? How would anger be dealt with? How might we rethink old age and death?

U

We may be tempted to dismiss emotional utopian thinking as ridiculously disconnected from the real world and therefore a waste of time. But Utopias are better understood as thought experiments in which we try to define important goals without having to bother with many of the practical issues that will one day have to be sorted out. We need our imaginations to go ahead and define a destination in order to know where we will have to direct our slow-moving packhorses and mules.

To the utopian thinker, the fact that we don't quite know every detail about how to carry out an important project doesn't constitute a decisive objection against it. A Utopia is what sets our course and defines our ambitions.

See also: Advertising; Envy of the Future; Good Business; Good Demand; Monasteries; State Broadcasting.

¶ Vocation Myth

The Vocation Myth is the belief in the spontaneous revelation of our professional destiny: we'll simply know in time what we need to do work-wise.

The difficulty of defining a professional goal currently lacks the generous, extensive and careful consideration it deserves. We tend to see confusion about our career paths as a slightly embarrassing failing that reflects poorly on its sufferers. Confusion is taken as a sign of being a bit muddled and impractical, of being unreasonably picky or hard to please;

perhaps we regard it as a consequence of being spoilt ('you should be thankful for any job') or as a troubling symptom of a lack of commitment or general flightiness. We arrive at these rather harsh assessments because we're still under the spell of a big and often poisonous idea that can be termed the Vocation Myth.

This myth originated around certain religious experiences, which, although rare, were regarded as hugely impressive and significant, and were accorded an inordinate degree of publicity in the history of the West. These were moments when an individual was summoned by God – sometimes speaking through an angel; at other points talking directly through the clouds – and was directed by God to devote their life to an aspect of the divine cause.

One significant story concerned the philosopher St. Augustine, who, in mid-life, changed jobs under divine instruction. He went from being a pagan professor of literature to being a Catholic bishop. It was a huge career change, but Augustine didn't have to work it out on his own. In 386, he happened to be staying in Milan and one day went out for a walk. He heard a child singing a lovely song he'd never heard before. The words of the chorus were 'pick it up, pick it up', and he understood that the words were a command from God. He was to pick up a Bible and read the first passage he set his eyes on. The very one he alighted upon told him to change his life and become the figure we know today as a great Catholic thinker and clergyman.

However tied to Catholic theology the story might seem, we have secularised such accounts without quite realising it. We too proceed as if, at some point, we might be expected to hear a quasi-celestial command directing us towards our life's purpose.

As often happens, it started with artists. Up until the Renaissance, being an artist was simply a kind of job that some people had, almost always because it was something that their father or uncle was involved in. Being a painter or making statues wasn't regarded as radically different from making shoes or bridles for horses; it was just a useful skilled trade that any assiduous individual who went through the proper course of training could become good at with time. But then, borrowing from the religious stories, artists began to think of themselves as 'called' by fate to a particular line of work. Something within them was pulling them towards their art. Michelangelo was the most extreme example of this attitude, seeing himself as required by his soul to paint fresco ceilings and chip away at blocks of marble. He might sometimes have wished he could stop, but he could only have done so by betraying his vocation.

The notion of vocation features in the biographies of many of the world's most famous people. For example, we learn that the pioneering French scientist Marie Curie knew from the age of fifteen that her life depended on being able to undertake scientific research. She struggled determinedly against every difficulty in her path – she had no money and when she was a student she nearly froze to death one winter and frequently fainted from hunger. But eventually she triumphed and was awarded two Nobel prizes, the first in 1903 for her work on X-rays and the second in 1911 for the discovery of radium and polonium.

As a result of such cases, having a vocation has come to seem a sure sign of being destined for great things. Conversely, to lack a vocation has come to seem not only a misfortune, but also the mark of inferiority. We end up not only panicked that we don't have a path in mind, but dispirited that our ignorance is proof that any path we do end up with will necessarily be an insignificant one.

What is worse, 'finding one's vocation' has come to seem like a discovery of which we should all be capable in a brief span of time. And the way to discover such a vocation should be (thanks to religious and artistic forerunners) entirely passive: one should simply wait for a moment of revelation, for the modern equivalent of a clap of thunder or a divine voice, an inner urge or an instinct pushing us towards podiatry or supply chain management.

A small but significant echo of this attitude can be traced in our habit of asking even very young children what they want to be when they are grown up. There's a faint but revealing assumption that somewhere among the options being entertained by the child (footballer, zookeeper, space explorer, etc.), there will already be the first stumbling articulations of the crucial inner voice announcing the small person's true destiny. It appears not to strike us as especially peculiar to expect a five-and-a-half-year-old to understand their identity in the adult labour market.

All this helps to explain the relative societal silence around the task of working out what to do with our lives. Well-meaning friends and family will often simply advise a confused person to wait, until one day something will strike them as just right.

Of course, contrary to what this unfortunate, oppressive notion of vocation suggests, it is entirely reasonable – even healthy – not to know what one's talents are or how to apply them. One's nature is ultimately so complex, one's abilities so tricky to define in detail, the needs of the world so elusive, that discovering the best fit between oneself and a job is a momentous, highly legitimate challenge that requires an immense amount of thought, exploration and wise assistance that might take up years of our attention. It's wholly reasonable not to know what work one should perform. Indeed, it is often a great sign of maturity to realise that one doesn't know rather than suffer any longer under the punishing assumption of innate vocation.

See also: Duty Trap, The; Job Fixation; Meaningful Work.

V

¶ Vulnerability

There are aspects to all of us that, if they were exposed to a harsh or unsympathetic critic, would result in severe humiliation and mockery.

From close up, none of us are reliably impressive. We get agitated, fretful, cantankerous and panicky. Under the pressure of events, we shout, slam doors and let out screams or wails. We have episodes of absurd clumsiness; we bump into doors, trip, and drop things down our front. We're worried pretty much all the time: about how others see us; about where our careers are going; about everything important that we have forgotten to do in our lives. We long for love, but are unthinking and insensitive around those close to us. We are gauche in our efforts to seduce and pitiful in our requests for attention. Our bodies have a range of shameful habits and vulnerabilities. We are, from certain angles, truly embarrassing propositions.

All this we struggle to hide. The Inner Idiot is carefully monitored and ruthlessly gagged. We have learnt from our earliest years that the only priority around vulnerability is to disguise it completely. We strive remorselessly to look composed, to erase the evidence of our silliness and to try to appear a great deal more 'normal' than we know we are.

We are understandably very focused on the downsides of vulnerability. What is far less well recognised is vulnerability's occasional significant and profound upsides.

There are moments when the revelation of weakness, far from being a catastrophe, is the only possible route to connection and respect. At points we may dare to explain, with rare frankness, that we are afraid, that we are sometimes bad and that we have done many silly things. Rather than appalling our companions, these revelations may serve to endear us to them, humanising us in their eyes, and letting them feel that their own vulnerabilities have echoes in the lives of others. Together, we realise that the definition of what is normal has missed out on key aspects of our mutual reality.

In other words, vulnerability can be the bedrock of friendship – friendship properly understood, not primarily as a process of admiration, but as an exchange of sympathy and consolation for the troublesome business of being alive.

There can, of course, be unfortunate ways of handling vulnerability: when we do so in the form of an aggressive demand that others rescue us, or when our frailties lack boundaries, or when we are close to rage and hysteria rather than melancholy and grief.

Good vulnerability doesn't expect another person to solve our difficulties; we let them see a tricky part of who we are, simply in the hope that they will be emboldened to feel more at ease with their own, less dignified sides. Good vulnerability is fundamentally generous: it takes the first step at disclosure so as to render it safe for others to unburden themselves and disclose something of their hidden selves in turn. It is a gift in the form of a risk taken for someone else.

Furthermore, displays of vulnerability have a curious way of signalling that we are, despite the embarrassing avowals, far from fundamentally ridiculous or pitiful. We are, rather, strong enough to be weak; to let our silliness, idiocy, anger and sadness show, confident that these do not have to be the final verdicts on who we are. We proceed with a bold sense that, despite the lack of surface evidence, everyone else is as wounded, aggrieved, worried and damaged as we are and that we are not therefore, through our disclosures, casting ourselves out of the clan for good: we are simply reconfirming our essential membership of the human race.

It is a minor tragedy that we should spend so much of our lives striving to hide our weakness when it is only upon the dignified sharing of vulnerability that true friendship and love can arise.

See also: Clumsiness; Inner Idiot, The; Jolliness; Melancholy; Normality; Politeness; Psychological Asymmetry; Sane Insanity; Warmth.

W

¶ Warmth

Although politeness is always preferable to rudeness, there are ways of being polite that badly miss the mark and can leave us, as its recipients, feeling oddly detached and dissatisfied. Picture the person who ends up, despite their best efforts, seeming what we can call 'coldly' polite. They may be extremely keen to please those they are seeing, they obey all the rules of etiquette, yet never manage to make their hospitality feel engaging or memorable. It may be a long time before another meeting with them is suggested.

By contrast, there is the person who exhibits the virtue of 'warmth'; someone who follows the cold person in the basic principles of politeness, but manages to add a critical emotionally comforting ingredient to their manner. When we have an evening planned with them, they might suggest making toasted cheese sandwiches at their place rather than going out to a restaurant; they might chat to us through the bathroom door, put on the songs they loved dancing to when they were fourteen, plump up a cushion and slot it behind our back, confess to feeling intimidated by a mutual acquaintance, bring us a posy of daisies or a card they made and, when we're down with the flu, call us up and ask how our ears are feeling.

The difference between the warm and the cold person lies in a contrasting vision of human nature. Broadly, the cold person is operating with an implicit view that those they are attempting to please are creatures endowed only with the highest needs. As a result, all kinds of assumptions are made about them: that they are interested exclusively in so-called serious topics (especially art and politics); that they will appreciate a degree of formality in dining and sitting; that they will be strong, self-contained and mature enough not to have any hunger for reassurance or cosiness, and that they will be without urgent physical vulnerabilities and drives that might prove offensive if they were mentioned.

Conversely, the warm person is always aware that the stranger is (irrespective of their status or outward dignity) a highly needy, fragile, confused, appetitive and susceptible creature. They know this about the stranger because they never forget this about themselves.

They know that however solid and dignified someone appears on the outside, behind the scenes there will inevitably be a struggling self, potentially awkward, easily bemused, beset by physical appetites, on the verge of loneliness, and frequently in need of nothing more subtle or elevated than a cheese sandwich, a glass of milk and a hug.

In a warm social manner we're catching sight of a major theme: the lower and 'bad' parts of a person are accepted and integrated into a more accurate picture of who they are. Warmth is a central way in which we get closer to other people through a due understanding of our collective human nature and thereby reduce the burdens of loneliness.

See also: Getting an Early Night; Listening as Editing; Loneliness; Normality; Shyness; Vulnerability.

¶ **Water Towers**

Our culture gives us ideas about what kinds of things might be worth admiring; it sends out hints about what is potentially fascinating, exciting, impressive or beautiful. But, in general, our current culture has had quite a restricted agenda. It has been very good at getting us to see the charms of dolphins,

W

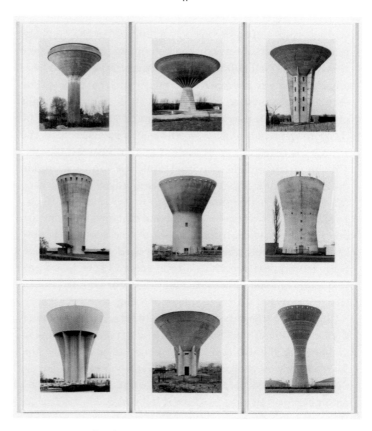

Bernd and Hilla Becher, *Water Towers*, 1972–2009.
The Bechers' sympathetic eye transformed water towers from unloved industrial
eyesores to objects worthy of admiration; art can do this for many under-appreciated
subjects in the world.

mountains, little villages in rural France, beaches with palm
trees, brilliantly engineered bridges and Art Deco hotels from
the 1920s. These are all worthy objects of delight, but they are
rare, which is a problem: the things we encounter every day
can feel dreary and disappointing by comparison.

In 1972, a German couple, Bernd and Hilla Becher, set
out to change these assumptions. They started to photograph

water towers across Germany and the US. These industrial structures were then among the least admired of all buildings; they were deemed hulking and brutish and people would become predictably furious if ever one was planned near where they lived

Yet the Bechers' photographs – arranged in serene and elegant frames, and hung in sequences along gallery walls – showed for the first time just how beautiful these towers actually were. One could appreciate the patterns of rust and their rugged authenticity; their legs had a certain dignity and playfulness.

The real point of the Bechers' exercise, however, wasn't specifically about water storage facilities. The towers provided an example for a much wider point: that there is a great deal more that is lovely and interesting in the world than we expect. To gain access to this, we may need some prompts and guidance. In other words, we may need art.

See also: Appreciation; Art, The Purpose of; Rock Appreciation; Small Pleasures.

¶ Weakness of Strength

The failings of friends, colleagues and partners can be deeply galling. We look upon their faults and wonder why they are the way they are.

At moments of particularly acute agitation, we need to rehearse the Weakness of Strength Theory. This dictates that we should strive to see people's weaknesses as the inevitable downside of certain merits that drew us to them, and from which we will benefit at other points – even if none of these benefits are apparent at present. What we're seeing are not their faults, pure and simple, but rather the shadow side of things that are genuinely good about them. We're picking up on weaknesses that derive from strengths.

W

In the 1870s, when he was living in Paris, the American novelist Henry James became a good friend of the celebrated Russian novelist Ivan Turgenev, who was also living in the city at that time. Henry James was particularly taken by the unhurried, tranquil style of the Russian writer's storytelling. He obviously took a long time over every sentence, weighing different options, changing and polishing until everything was perfect. It was an ambitious, inspiring approach to writing.

However, in personal and social life, these same virtues could make Turgenev a maddening companion. He would accept an invitation to lunch, then, the day before, send a note explaining that he would not be able to attend, then another saying how much he looked forward to the occasion. Then he would turn up – two hours late. Arranging anything with him was a nightmare. Yet his social waywardness was really just the same thing that made him so attractive as a writer. It was the same unwillingness to hurry; the same desire to keep the options open until the last moment. This produced marvellous books, but dinner party chaos. In reflecting on Turgenev's character, Henry James reflected that his Russian friend was exhibiting the 'weakness of his strength'.

The theory goes like this: every strength that an individual has necessarily brings with it a weakness of which it is an inherent part. It is impossible to have strengths without weaknesses. Every virtue has an associated weakness. Not all the virtues can belong together in a single person.

This is a theory that can help calm us down at moments of particular crisis, because it changes the way we see the defects, failings and weakness of others. Our minds tend to hive off the strengths and see these as essential, while deeming the weaknesses as a freakish add-on; in truth, the weaknesses are part and parcel of the strengths.

The theory usefully undermines the unhelpful idea that – if only we looked a bit harder – we would find someone who was always perfect to be around. If strengths are invariably connected to failings, there won't be anyone who is remotely flawless. We may well find people with different strengths, but they will also have a new litany of weaknesses.

See also: Charity of Interpretation; Love as Generosity; Splitting and Integration; Universal Love.

¶ Wisdom

To teach us how to be wise is the underlying central purpose of philosophy. The word may sound abstract and lofty, but wisdom is something we might plausibly aim to acquire a little more of over the course of our lives, even if true wisdom requires that we always keep in mind the persistent risk of madness and error.

Wisdom can be said to comprise twelve ingredients:

Realism
The wise are, first and foremost, 'realistic' about how challenging many things can be. They are fully conscious of the complexities entailed in any project: raising a child, starting a business, spending an agreeable weekend with the family, changing the nation, falling in love … Knowing that something difficult is being attempted doesn't rob the wise of ambition, but it makes them more steadfast, calmer and less prone to panic about the problems that will invariably come their way. The wise rarely expect anything to be wholly easy or to go entirely well.

Gratitude
Properly aware that much can and will go wrong, the wise are unusually alive to moments of calm and beauty, even extremely modest ones, of the kind that those with grander plans rush past. With the dangers and tragedies of existence

firmly in mind, they can take pleasure in a single, uneventful, sunny day, or some pretty flowers growing by a brick wall, the charm of a three-year-old playing in a garden, or an evening of intimate conversation among friends. It isn't that they are sentimental and naive, but precisely the opposite: they have seen how hard things can get, and they know how to draw the full value from the peaceful and the sweet – whenever and wherever these arise.

Folly

The wise know that all human beings, themselves included, are never far from folly: they have irrational desires and incompatible aims; they are unaware of much of what they feel; they are prone to mood swings; they are visited by powerful fantasies and delusions; they are buffeted by the curious demands of their sexuality. The wise are unsurprised by the ongoing co-existence of deep immaturity and perversity alongside quite adult qualities such as intelligence and morality. They know that we are barely evolved apes. Aware that at least half of life is irrational, they try wherever possible to budget for madness and are slow to panic when it (reliably) rears its head.

Humour

The wise take seriously the business of laughing at themselves. They hedge their pronouncements and are sceptical in their conclusions. Their certainties are not as brittle as those of others. They laugh due to the constant collisions between the noble way they would like things to be and the demented way they often turn out.

Politeness

The wise are realistic about social relations – in particular, about how difficult it is to change people's minds and have an effect on their lives. They are therefore extremely reticent about telling others too frankly what they think. They have a sense of how seldom it is useful to get censorious with others. Above all, they want things to be nice in social settings, even if this means they are not totally authentic. They will sit with someone of an opposite political persuasion and not try to convert them; they will hold their tongue at someone who seems to be announcing a wrong-headed plan for reforming the country, educating their child or directing their personal life. They'll be aware of how differently things can look through the eyes of others and will search more for what people have in common than what separates them.

Self-acceptance

The wise have made their peace with the yawning gap between how they ideally want to be and what they are actually like. They have come to terms with their tendencies to idiocy, ugliness and error. They are not fundamentally ashamed of themselves because they have already shed so much of their pride.

Forgiveness

The wise are comparably realistic about other people. They recognise the extraordinary pressures everyone is under to pursue their own ambitions, defend their interests and seek their own pleasures. It can make others appear extremely 'mean' and purposefully evil, but this would be to over-personalise the issue. The wise know that most hurt is unintentional – it's a by-product of the constant collision of competing egos in a world of scarce resources.

The wise are therefore slow to anger and judgement. They don't leap to the worst conclusions about what is going on in the minds of others. They will be readier to overlook a hurt from a proper sense of how difficult every life is, harbouring as it does so many frustrated ambitions, disappointments and longings. The wise appreciate the pressures people are under. Of course they shouted, of course they were rude, naturally they want to appear as slightly more important than they

W

are ... The wise are generous in seeing the reasons why people might not be nice. They feel less persecuted by the aggression and meanness of others, because they have a sense of where it comes from: a place of hurt.

Resilience

The wise have a solid sense of what they can survive. They know just how much can go wrong and yet things will still be (just about) liveable. The unwise person draws the boundaries of their contentment too far out, so that it encompasses, and depends upon, fame, money, personal relationships, popularity, health ... The wise person sees the advantages of all of these, but also knows that they may – before too long, at a time of fate's choosing – have to draw the borders right back and find contentment within a more bounded space.

Envy

The wise person doesn't envy idly: they realise that there are some good reasons why they don't have many of the things they really want. They look at the tycoon or the star and have a decent grasp of why they weren't able to succeed at this level. It looks like an accident – an unfair one – but there were in fact some logical grounds.

At the same time, the wise see that some destinies are truly shaped by nothing more than accident. Some people are promoted randomly. Companies that aren't especially deserving can suddenly make it big. Some people have the right parents. The winners aren't all noble and good. The wise appreciate the role of luck and don't curse themselves overly at those junctures where they have not had as much of it as they would have liked.

Success and Failure

The wise emerge as realistic about the consequences of winning and succeeding. They may want to win as much as the next person, but they are aware of how many fundamentals will remain unchanged whatever the outcome. They don't exaggerate the transformations available to us. They know how much we remain tethered to some basic dynamics in our personalities, whatever job we have or whatever material possession we acquire. This is both cautionary (for those who succeed) and hopeful (for those who won't). The wise see the continuities across those two categories over-emphasised by modern consumer capitalism: 'success' and 'failure'.

Regrets

In our ambitious age, it is common to begin with dreams of being able to pull off an unblemished life, where one can hope to get the major decisions in love and work right.

But the wise realise that it is impossible to fashion a spotless life; everyone will make large and uncorrectable errors in a number of areas. Perfectionism is a wicked illusion. Regret is unavoidable.

But regret lessens the more we see that error is endemic across the species. One can't look at anyone's life story without seeing some devastating mistakes etched across it. These errors are not coincidental but structural; they arise because we all lack the information we need to make choices in time-sensitive situations. Where it counts, we are all steering almost blind.

Calm

The wise know that turmoil is always around the corner, and they have come to fear and sense its approach. That's why they nurture such a strong commitment to calm. A quiet evening feels like an achievement. A day without anxiety is something to be celebrated. They are not afraid of having a somewhat boring time. Things could be, and will be again, so much worse.

W

Finally, of course, the wise know that it will never be possible to be wise every hour, let alone every day, of their lives.

See also: Akrasia; Emotional Education; Emotional Intelligence; Faulty Walnut, The; Glamour; Good Enough; Philosophical Meditation; Philosophy; Splitting and Integration; Success at School vs. Success in Life.

¶ Work/Life Balance

We have formed ever-higher expectations about what it means to be a good parent in exactly the same historical epoch in which the importance of work has been stressed as never before. The demands of the labour market have not been offset by any reduction in the expectations around intimacy, devotion or time in the home. We are under more pressure to succeed at work and under more pressure to be very continually present and focused domestically.

The notion of 'balance' has been, rather cruelly, proposed to solve the problem. But the truth is that we can rarely contrive a just accommodation between competing demands. By definition, any worthwhile project will unbalance our lives and demand too much of us. We'd understand the impossibility of society routinely asking us to become experts at chess while also holding down a career as a rally car driver. It is not the fault of the world, or of ourselves, that we don't see that we are asking ourselves something very similar on a routine basis. Not all good ideals are compatible. A society cannot be highly democratic and highly rational at the same time; a business cannot be daringly innovative and a rock-solid investment. And we cannot be perfect parents and perfect workers. We can, at best, hope to be good enough.

See also: Expectations; Good Enough; Meaningful Work.

Thematic Index

1. Self-Knowledge

2. Other People

3. Relationships

4. Sexuality

7. Culture

8. Religion

Picture Credits

p.26   Christen Købke, *View of a Street in Østerbro outside Copenhagen.*
         Morning Light, 1836.
         Oil on canvas, 106.5 × 161.5 cm
         Statens Museum for Kunst, Denmark
         The Artchives / Alamy Stock Photo

p.36   John Pawson, *The Life House*, Wales, 2016
         © Gilbert McCarragher

p.37   Church of Santa Prisca, Taxco, Mexico. Constructed 1751–1758.
         age fotostock / Alamy Stock Photo

p.38   Edmund Blair Leighton, *The End of The Song*, 1902
         Oil on canvas, 128.5 × 147.3 cm
         Private Collection
         Art Collection 2 / Alamy Stock Photo

p.38   Jacques-Louis David, *The Oath of the Horatii*, 1784
         Oil on canvas, 330 × 425 cm
         The Louvre, Paris
         Artepics / Alamy Stock Photo

p.41   Caspar Netscher, *The Lacemaker*, 1662
         Oil on canvas: 33 × 27 cm
         © The Wallace Collection, London

p.70   The Great Hall, Rijksmuseum, Amsterdam, 2013
         Photographer: René den Engelsman, 2013
         Courtesy of Rijksmuseum, Amsterdam

p.69   The British Library Reading Room, British Museum, London, 1857.
         Before restoration.
         Architect: Sydney Smirke
         Arcaid Images / Alamy Stock Photo

p.107   Sir David Wilkie, *George IV (1762–1830)*, 1829
         Oil on canvas, 279.4 × 179.1 cm
         Royal Collection Trust/© Her Majesty Queen Elizabeth II 2017

p.120   Ludolf Bakhuizen, *Warships in a Heavy Storm*, c.1695
         Oil on canvas, 150 × 227 cm
         Purchased with the support of the Vereniging Rembrandt.
         Courtesy Rijksmuseum, Amsterdam

p.137   Tea bowl, Joseon period, early 17th century
         Porcelain with translucent glaze; gold lacquer repairs, 5.9 × 11.7 cm
         ACCESSION NUMBER F1904.318
         Gift of Charles Lang Freer
         © Freer Gallery of Art

p.200   (top) Guo Xu, Mi Fu Honoring a Rock, 1503
        Album of eleven leaves; ink and colours on paper, 29.8 × 49.3 cm
        Shanghai Museum, China

        (bottom) Gongshi or Scholar's Rock,
        Based Xinjiang Province, China
        Indeterminate Age
        Huang Lai (Jade) Stone, 10.2 x 10.2 x 20.3 cm
        Photo courtesy of Primitive, Inc.; I.D. #A0910-155; www.beprimitive.com

p.202   Eugène Delacroix, *Liberty Leading the People*, 1830.
        Oil on canvas, 260 × 325 cm
        The Louvre, Paris
        North Wind Picture Archives / Alamy Stock Photo

p.213   Michelangelo, *David*, 1501–04
        Marble, height 408 cm
        Galleria dell'Accademia, Florence
        muratart/Shutterstock.com

p.214   Altar in the pilgrimage church of the Fourteen Holy Saints, Wallfahrtskirche
        Vierzehnheiligen, Bavaria. Constructed 1743–1772.
        LOOK Die Bildagentur der Fotografen GmbH / Alamy Stock Photo

p.264   Bernd and Hilla Becher, *Water Towers*, 1972–2009
        Nine photographs, gelatin silver print on paper. Displayed: 172 x 142 cm
        © Estate of Bernd Becher & Hilla Becher
        Photo Credit: © Tate, London 2017.

The School of Life is dedicated to developing emotional intelligence – believing that a range of our most persistent problems are created by a lack of self-understanding, compassion and communication. We operate from ten physical campuses around the world, including London, Amsterdam, Seoul and Melbourne. We produce films, run classes, offer therapy and make a range of psychological products. **The School of Life Press** publishes books on the most important issues of emotional life. Our titles are designed to entertain, educate, console and transform.